KT-454-491

CONTENTS

5

Part Three: Responding to Racism

EDITORS AND CONTRIBUTORS

The Editors

Fintan Farrell is a founder member of the Irish Traveller Movement (ITM) where he is now employed as policy officer. He was part of the Community Platform team that negotiated the Programme for Prosperity and Fairness, and is a past president of the European Anti-Poverty Network, based in Brussels. He has considerable experience in highlighting and campaigning against racism.

Philip Watt is Director of the National Consultative Committee on Racism and Interculturalism (NCCRI), which is an advisory body established by the Minister for Justice, Equality and Law Reform in July 1998. He has edited a number of publications on racism and social exclusion related issues, published by the European Parliament Office, ADM, and Government Stationery Office.

The Contributors

Tania Kaur McFarland is a representative from the Indian community in Ireland within the context of the EU Migrants Forum. Brought up and educated in Malaysia of Sikh parents, and now an Irish Citizen, she has considerable direct experience of the policies, and treatment of foreign workers, in many different countries, including Ireland.

Martin Collins is a Traveller and is deputy director of Pavee Point, the Traveller's Centre based in Dublin. He has considerable experience in campaigning against racism and in promoting Travellers' rights. Martin has recently been appointed to the newly established Human Rights Commission and has been a member of the board of the NCCRI since it was established.

Jean Pierre Eyanga is a member of the Congo Solidarity Group and a refugee who worked for a number of years to highlight the needs and rights of refugees and asylum-seekers in Ireland. He is by profession a Veterinary Surgeon. He has spoken at many seminars and conferences on racism and the experience of being a refugee.

Rose Tuelo Brock is originally from South Africa and now lives in Galway where she is a member of Galway One World and Women from Minorities in Europe. She is a freelance journalist and a winner of a media award for her work in highlighting racism during the European Year Against Racism (1997). She has also tutored on issues such as aid, debt and how the Third World is presented in the media.

Piaras Mac Éinrí has been Director of the Irish Centre for Migration Studies at NUI Cork since it was established in 1997. He is a former First Secretary in the Department of Foreign Affairs. He has written extensively on migration and related issues and has been published widely in international and Irish journals and books. He has also been involved in the work of NASC, based in Cork

Anastasia Crickley is a lecturer in the Applied Social Studies Centre in NUI Maynooth, chairperson of the NCCRI, and former chairperson of the National Coordinating Committee for European Year Against Racism (1997). She has written extensively on issues such as racism, women and local and community development, and has been actively involved in campaigning on Travellers' issues for many years.

Ronnie Fay is Director of Pavee Point, the Travellers Centre based in Dublin. She was a founder member of the Pavee Point Primary Health Care Programme, which is widely recognised as an innovative and participative model of primary health care in Ireland. She is involved in the Community Platform in issues related to social partnership and has campaigned for the more effective application of EU structural funding in tackling inequality and social exclusion.

Donal O'Loingsigh has been actively involved in the Trade Union movement for many years and has just completed his term as President of the Irish National Teachers Organisation, the largest teacher's union in Ireland. Through the INTO he has actively worked to ensure that Ireland's education system and structures are open to building a more inclusive and intercultural approach to the needs of minority ethnic groups.

Nuala Haughey is Social and Racial Affairs Correspondent with the *Irish Times* and has written extensively on the broader issue of racism and, in particular, on issues related to asylum and immigration. She is a graduate of the journalism course in Dublin City University and has a background in legal issues.

Hugh Frazer is a national expert working with the EU Commission on issues of poverty and social exclusion. He was formerly Director of the Combat Poverty Agency and the Northern Ireland Voluntary Trust. He has written extensively on poverty and social exclusion in Ireland.

Kensika Monshengwo is training and resource officer with the National Consultative Committee on Racism and Interculturalism (NCCRI). He was born in Zaire and is a post-graduate from the Sorbonne in Paris. He is chairperson of the Congo Solidarity Group and the Association of Refugees and Asylum Seekers in Ireland (ARASI).

Fr Donal O'Mahony is a Capuchin Priest who has worked and written on social justice issues for many years. He formerly worked with Threshold, the organisation that works for justice on housing and homelessness throughout Ireland.

Niall Crowley is Chief Executive Officer of the Equality Authority, which is the body that oversees the implementation of the Equality Legislation (the Employment Equality Act and the Equal Status Act). He previously worked as Director of Pavee Point Travellers Centre, which is based in Dublin. He has written and worked to highlight the issue of racism for many years.

PART ONE

RESPONDING TO RACISM IN IRELAND: AN OVERVIEW

Fintan Farrell and Philip Watt

Introduction

EVEN THE USE of the term 'racism' continues to evoke a wide range of different, and sometimes opposing, reactions and responses. Until recently, one of the most common responses was to deny that racism was a problem in Ireland. This is perhaps one of the factors that has contributed to a lack of debate and dialogue on the issue.

Another commonly articulated view was that if groups did experience racism in Ireland, it was somehow their own fault arising either from some form of deficiency on their part and/or the failure of such groups, in particular the Traveller community, to allow themselves to be subsumed into Irish society.

Complacency and denial also influenced political approaches to the issue of tackling racism in Ireland, which was highlighted by the failure of successive governments in Ireland to ratify the International Convention on the Elimination of all Forms of Racial Discrimination until January 2001, some thirty-two years after it was first promulgated by the United Nations.

The range of measures introduced at a national level in recent years, some of which are highlighted in this publication, is evidence that racism is now a much more important public policy concern. The reasons for this change have been as a consequence of a number of interlinked factors. These include the ongoing work of non-government organisations, in particular Traveller, refugee, asylum and human rights organisations, and trade unions, in highlighting the issue and their lobbying for legislation and policy changes. The media has also played an important role in highlighting issues of concern, including a perceived increase in racist incidents, such as physical assaults. More recently there has been a concern from the business and employer sector that racism could have a strong and detrimental effect on growth levels in the economy and could act as a deterrent in attracting and retaining non-EU workers to fill significant skills and labour shortages.

In recent years there has been the commencement of a public debate and dialogue about racism in Ireland. To date, this debate has been robust – and at times conflictual – but has generally been constructive and has sought to move the issues forward. However, the denial of racism continues to persist. It remains a matter of concern that some important opinion formers, particularly in some sectors of the media, continue to be dismissive about the need to address racism.

The public debate has also tended to be limited in scope, with racism sometimes reduced to, or equated with, a discourse concerning issues around immigration and refugee and asylum policy. Many of the contributions to this book acknowledge the centrality of these issues to the present debate, but the scope and diversity of the themes covered in this publication demonstrate that a narrow focus on these policy issues on their own will only reveal an incomplete picture.

Reducing a discussion on racism to a discussion on migration and asylum policy can also have the, albeit often unintentional, effect of reinforcing the myth that the only people in Ireland to experience racism are recent migrants and that ethnic and cultural diversity in Ireland is as a consequence of recent migration. This myth is implicitly and explicitly challenged in a number of contributions to this book. It is increasingly becoming acknowledged that there are different forms of racism in Ireland, which have been identified as[1]:

- racism experienced by Travellers on the basis of their distinct ethnic and nomadic identity.
- racism experienced by refugees and asylum-seekers.
- racism experienced by black and minority ethnic groups on the basis of their skin colour and ethnic identity.
- racism experienced by, and potential exploitation of, migrant workers.
- the particular forms of racism experienced by women from minority ethnic groups.

The blaming of minority ethnic groups for creating racism in Ireland and the adoption of racist slogans such as 'Ireland for the Irish' by a small number of individuals and groups in Ireland has a resonance with the language adopted by the far right in other European countries. In many countries in Europe there has been a worrying increase in the electoral support for political parties that advocate policies against minority ethnic groups and diversity, and seek to implement repressive immigration and asylum policies and dismantle or restrict equality and anti-racism measures.

To date, there have only been a few examples of groups or individuals openly advocating neo-racist positions in Ireland. Without engendering a sense of complacency, the direct support and credibility of these individuals and groups have been relatively limited, even if others would privately share some of their views.

It is to be welcomed that there is a broad consensus within the main political parties in Ireland to address racism. All the parties represented in the Oireachtas have recently signed an anti-racism protocol that commits them to sending a clear and positive message to their constituents that they reject racism.

The potential for racism to be perpetuated through the systems or structures of institutions is beginning to receive attention in Ireland. A number of statutory institutions are aware of this potential and are actively adopting anti-racism training modules for staff and bringing in anti-racism commitments as part of a broader approach to equality.

The importance of collecting data is crucial in identifying where remedial action needs to be taken, and in tackling discrimination in areas such as the provision and impact of services, and the recruitment, promotion and retention of staff in the workplace. Many non-government organisations now advocate that statutory institutions need to go further and provide a leadership role, and that the government should bring in a statutory duty to promote equality throughout the public service, as is the case in Britain and Northern Ireland.

Aims of this book
This book seeks to contribute to the public debate and dialogue, and to act as a catalyst for further discourse on the issue of racism in Ireland. There are three aims to this book, which also inform its structure. The first aim is to provide an accessible guide to the some of the key concepts and terms related to racism and anti-racism, including an explanation of the main terms that are used in this book and in the wider debate on racism and anti-racism

The second aim is to provide some insights from those who experience racism in Ireland and from those who have direct personal and/or professional experience in responding to racism in areas such as health and education. This section also looks at how the analysis of this experience is now informing responses to racism.

The third aim is to examine some of the emerging responses to racism by both government and non-government organisations, not as a complacent checklist about what has been achieved, but to provide the basis for strengthened and additional measures to address racism in the future.

The book brings together a wide range of contributors, including academics, journalists, trade unionists, Church leaders, community workers and those working in specialised agencies with a remit to respond to racism. The overall approach adopted by the editors has been to seek contributions that are critical, but also constructive and forward looking and which will contribute to the debate on how to tackle racism, rather than simply restating the problems.

Summary and structure

The following section is a summary of some of the main issues that have been highlighted by the contributors to this book.

Part One: Overview

The book is divided into three sections. This overview section concludes with an accessible guide and critique to the key language and concepts in relation to racism.

Part Two: The Context

Section Two looks at the experience of racism and how this experience has been developed into an analysis that has informed responses to racism. As outlined earlier in this section, there are different forms of racism in Ireland, some of which are addressed in this section of the publication. Tania

Kaur McFarland from the EU Migrants Forum and the India Club addresses the issues facing migrants living in Ireland, their concerns about the burden imposed by the level of regulation and bureaucracy, and the potential for such regulation to be construed as a form of discrimination. She concludes by urging that, rather than responding when some national crisis occurs, 'what we need now is to have a vision of what our society should be like in the future. It appears that the world is moving towards a high degree of racial and ethnic integration and Ireland cannot escape that reality.'

Martin Collins, of Pavee Point Travellers Centre, a member of the Board of the NCCRI and the Human Rights Commission, outlines the socio-economic circumstances of Irish Travellers and concerns about the pace of change, despite recent advances in policy. He identifies the need to promote greater solidarity between Gypsies, Roma and Travellers at European level and within Ireland. He refers to the growing acceptance of the concept of institutional discrimination, which can happen both intentionally and unintentionally: 'In our case, what this means is that services are designed by the majority population for the majority population'. He concludes by emphasising the role that non-government organisations have played in the fight against racism and the need to ensure that this role is adequately resourced.

Dr Jean Pierre Eyanga, a member of the Congo Solidarity Group, looks at the racism experienced by refugees and asylum-seekers and concludes that, while his experiences and the experiences of many other refugees and asylum-seekers in Ireland have been positive, there is increasing concern at a perceived resurgence in racism, including racially motivated violence. He urges that services provided by the State, including the Gardaí and school authorities, should be more responsive to the issues and concerns raised by refugees and asylum-seekers. He raises concerns about the provisions related to refugees and asylum-seekers in the new immigration legislation and hopes 'that the Irish Government will adopt the same urgency when it considers measures to protect the community against racism and xenophobia.'

Rose Tuelo Brock, originally from South Africa and now living in Galway, is a member of Galway One World and Women from Minorities in Europe. Rose Brock speaks from the perspective of the racism experienced by black people in Ireland, irrespective of their legal status, and in particular the racism experienced by black women. Her input also draws attention to the potential of racism in influencing our perceptions of 'developing countries'. She challenges the concept of 'toleration' as, 'in my opinion, when you tolerate something, it is because you are uncomfortable with it, uneasy and threatened... I do not want to be tolerated. I want to be affirmed and accepted because I have the right to be.'

Ireland has traditionally been a country of emigration. This has changed in the very recent past, as more migrants are needed to fill skills and labour shortages. At the same time, the country is also attracting increasing numbers of asylum-seekers and refugees. In a timely contribution, in the context of the review of immigration and residence policy announced by the Irish government in June 2001, Piaras Mac Éinrí from the Irish Centre for Migration studies provides an overview and critique of existing immigration and related policy in Ireland, including immigration flows, the regulatory framework for immigration, integration policy and the rights and protections afforded to migrant workers. He calls for urgent reform of the work permit system, better coordination between government departments on immigration, and for greater social as well as economic rights to be afforded to migrant workers on issues such as education, training and family reunification.

Women from minority ethnic groups can experience additional and specific forms of discrimination arising from the intersection between gender and racism. Anastasia Crickley, a lecturer in NUI Maynooth, looks at how this intersection can be experienced and at some of the issues this raises for feminists, anti-racist groups and those concerned with human rights and equality. She concludes by drawing out possible future strategies and actions and states: 'Not ignoring the racism experienced by women means naming it and addressing it not just in articles and publications on women and racism but in every article, action, discussion and strategy against racism.'

A central theme that emerges from this book is that tackling discrimination alone will only be a partial response to tackling racism. There is also a need to embrace and celebrate cultural and ethnic diversity and to reflect these principles in the approach we adopt to the type of services we provide. Donal O'Loingsigh, President of the Irish National Teachers Organisation but writing in a personal capacity, looks at the potential issues arising between increasing cultural diversity in Irish schools and the challenges that such diversity presents for an education system that is still largely delivered along denominational lines. He contends that schools that strive to create an environment in which the positive worth of the individual, both children and teachers, is valued and recognised are more likely to achieve the type of ethos necessary to tackle successfully the issues of racism and culture. He concludes that the creation of a truly intercultural education system demands both changes in approach and structural changes on how schools are established and managed.

Ronnie Fay, Director of Pavee Point Travellers Centre, contends that there is an urgent need to provide affirmative action in the provision of health care to Travellers to counter the unacceptably high sickness and mortality rates. Changing the health status of Travellers requires not just a health strategy, but must be integrated with adequate standards of accommodation, coordination between different services and a change of approach in how health care and services, are provided to the Traveller community. She concludes that while there have been some positive recent developments, such as the commitment to the Primary Health Care approach currently being developed by Pavee Point, future progress is largely dependent on a clear and agreed national policy on Travellers' health being fully implemented by the Department of Health and Children.

Part Three: Responding to Racism
The third section of the book deals with responding to racism. The first article in this section is by Nuala Haughey, a correspondent with the *Irish Times*, who looks at the role of the media in addressing racism. She contends that the failure of some sections of the media to live up to the standards set by the National Union of Journalists, and expected of them by society, has been well documented. Her article focuses on a range of possible remedies, including the establishment of a possible press ombudsman or a complaints commission to deal with readers complaints and to enforce a code of practice; awareness training for people working in the media industry; the adequate resourcing and support provided to support and community groups to enable them to get their message across more effectively.

Community development has a key role in tackling poverty and racism. Hugh Frazer, the Director of the Combat Poverty Agency, contends there is a complex and multi-faceted connection between racism and poverty. He identifies two key strategies to address this connection within the wider context of attitudinal and structural change in society: the fostering of

S0034425

AN LEABHARLANN
305 8

a community development approach and the mainstreaming of an anti-racism dimension in Ireland's (and Europe's) National Anti-Poverty Strategy and related government policies and programmes. All EU Member states are required to submit a national action plan against poverty and social exclusion to the EU Commission, and in Ireland there is currently a review of Ireland's National Anti-Poverty Strategy. These initiatives provide a key opportunity to ensure that racism as a cause of poverty is addressed and that minority ethnic groups are included and targeted in measures to address poverty and social exclusion.

Governments are increasingly promoting national public awareness programmes as important tools in the fight against racism. Kensika Monshengwo, training and resource officer with the National Consultative Committee on Racism and Interculturalism (NCCRI), looks at public awareness programmes that have been developed in Australia and Canada and, more recently, the approach advocated by the NCCRI to the government in relation to the forthcoming public awareness programme in Ireland. He concludes that to ensure the success of such programmes, they should be integrated into broader policies to address racism, they should have visible and high-level political support, and their planning should involve a broad consultation process. Public awareness programmes should be ambitious and seek to create the conditions for changes in behaviour, practice and policy, as well as changes in attitude, and there is a need to ensure that such programmes are not undermined by significant delays. 'The way that the programme is implemented will be key to its success; in particular it is important that the programme is perceived to be concerned with public awareness rather than public relations.'

The role of the Christian Churches in Ireland in combating

racism, with particular reference to refugees and asylum-seekers, is examined by Fr Donal O'Mahony OFM Cap. His chapter is divided into two sections. The first examines the issues from an 'earth perspective' theology; he challenges Churches to work in solidarity with refugees and to consider the issues from a more global perspective than they currently do. The second part looks at how the institutional Christian Churches are responding and concludes that there has been a positive response through the publication of submissions, the financial support of projects seeking to assist refugees and asylum-seekers and through education programmes. He emphasises the need for Irish Churches to work together with ecumenical endeavour and to contact and provide practical help to person of other faiths and for people to bear witness to their faith by actions. He concludes, 'so welcome the refugee as she or he passes through your parish or diocese. Our practical commitment to refugees, should become a test of the authenticity of our faith.'

In the final chapter Niall Crowley, CEO of the Equality Authority, outlines the key elements being developed through the emerging institutional framework to combat racism in Ireland and, in particular, the work of the Equality Authority. These elements include participation and agenda setting, mainstreaming and targeting, and institutions to drive forward such rights. He outlines some of the key initiatives undertaken by the Equality Authority towards these objectives and highlights the need for approaches emerging at national level to be replicated at local level and within individual institutions. He concludes by identifying the key elements that could inform a policy within an individual organisation, including an equality policy, a named person to ensure the implementation of policy, data collection and analysis.

Conclusion

In conclusion, this book marks one of the first widely published and accessible publications on racism in Ireland. The book is intended to be a catalyst for further debate and discussion, rather than an end in itself. A key feature of the contributions is that they are forward looking and constructive and serve to build a bridge between experience, context and the need to develop effective strategies to respond to racism.

Addressing discrimination against minority ethnic groups and building a more inclusive and intercultural society are, in effect, two sides of the one coin. At the very least, the basic human rights of people from minority ethnic groups in Ireland need effective protection, including ensuring equality in areas such as employment and the provision of goods and services. In this context, the development of recent legislation and policy in Ireland to address racism and promote equality should be acknowledged, not from a sense of complacency, but as the basis of renewing our combined efforts to respond to racism. This publication highlights the need for greater consistency in areas of related policy that impact directly on minority ethnic groups, including policies towards Travellers, immigration and residence policy and refugee and asylum policy. These will provide some of the tests to judge overall policy and institutional commitment to human rights, equality and anti-racism in Ireland.

There are a number of myths that have gained common currency, but which are effectively challenged in this publication, including:

• the myth that racism only began when asylum applications increased and Ireland became a country of inward migration, rather than emigration
• the tendency to deny that racism is a problem in Ireland and

to dismiss and label those who are concerned about the issue as being politically correct

- the myths perpetuated by labelling peoples and groups on the basis of negative characteristics
- the assumption that the racism experienced by women from minority ethnic groups is necessarily addressed in existing anti-racism strategies
- the myth that racism is simply about a set of beliefs and attitudes and prejudices, without recognising how beliefs and attitudes influence behaviour, actions and policy
- the myth that tackling racism can be resolved by education and public awareness alone without these potentially important strategies being integrated into a consistent and broader framework of policies and structures to tackle the issue

An accessible guide to key terms and concepts

The following is intended to be an accessible guide to the key concepts that are discussed in this book and the wider debate on racism. The use of language and the conceptual basis of racism has been an evolving process and is subject to ongoing debate. This guide seeks to highlight the most commonly used concepts and terms and to reflect the increasingly broad consensus about their meaning that has emerged in recent years.

Racism

The UNESCO and UN declarations on racism are the most widely acknowledged definitions of racism and give a clear statement that racism is without scientific foundation.

The UNESCO Declaration (1978) states:

> Any theory involving the claim that racial or ethnic groups are inherently superior or inferior, thus implying that some would be entitled to dominate or eliminate

others who would be inferior; or which places a value judgement on racial differentiation, has no scientific foundation and is contrary to the moral and ethical principles of humanity.

The UN international Convention on all Forms of Racist Discrimination (1969) states:

Any distinction, exclusion, restriction or preference, based on race, colour, descent, national or ethnic origin, which has the purpose of modifying or impairing the recognition, the enjoyment or exercise on an equal footing of human rights and fundamental freedom in the political, economic, social, cultural, or any other field of public life constitutes racial discrimination.

These internationally accepted definitions clearly indicate that racism is more than a set of attitudes or prejudice. Racism is a specific form of discrimination associated with skin colour and ethnicity. There is also a conscious or unconscious ideological basis to racism that involves superiority and a set of beliefs and processes to justify oppression against people of perceived different 'race' or ethnic origin. It also involves the abuse of power by one group over another group. So, while racism involves negative stereotypes and assumptions, it should not be reduced simply to attitudes, thereby equating it with prejudice. The reality of unequal power combined with prejudice enables some groups to treat others in racist ways by denying them access to opportunities, resources and decision-making processes.[2]

What is 'race' and why is it now a discredited term?
The term 'race' has been now been discredited as a residual concept from the nineteenth century when it was used to

define recognisable categories within the human species, in order to rank people according to physical and ideological criteria. The acceptance of 'race' as a credible concept has been used as a justification for racism, although as a term, 'race' is still used in both legal and other contexts in Ireland, North and South. It is now widely accepted that human beings are one species. Species is a biological term given to any group of animals or plants than can procreate and produce descendants. Within this species (*homo sapiens*) there is a diversity of physical features: skin colour, facial features, bone structures, hair, height and so on. The concept of ethnicity has largely replaced 'race'.

What is an ethnic group and ethnicity?
An ethnic group is a group of people sharing a collective identity based on a sense of common history and ancestry. Ethnic groups possess their own culture, customs, norms, beliefs and traditions. Other relevant characteristics shared in common could be language, geographical origin, literature, or religion. An ethnic group can be a majority or a minority group within a larger community. All people belong to one or more ethnic groups but we are often unaware of our ethnicity if we are part of the dominant ethnic group. Ethnicity is a cultural phenomenon that is distinct from the concept of 'race', which has a perceived biological basis. Culture is learned and passed on from generation to generation. Culture also evolves and changes and the recognition of this fluidity is important so as not to stereotype an ethnic group into one fixed set of expressions of its cultural identity. In a healthy society, changes in the cultural practices of an ethnic group would come from the experience within the ethnic group and from its interaction with other ethnic communities, as distinct from change that is forced on the ethnic group by the values and 'norms' of the dominant ethnic group in the society.

What is the potential impact of 'labelling'.

Labelling is a common process associated with racism that – either intentionally or unintentionally – attributes a set of perceived characteristics to an identifiable group. The labelling process can most usefully be detected over a course of time, for instance through the study of particular newspaper reports. The labelling process demonises and dehumanises people and, in the worst cases, can help to create the conditions that make discrimination and even violence against minority ethnic groups more acceptable. The most common forms of labelling against minority ethnic groups in Ireland has involved the exaggeration and sensationalising of numbers of people, through the use of emotive terms such as 'floods and tides'; the labelling of people as being 'scroungers' and out to abuse the social welfare system and the persistent association of people from minority ethnic groups with crime or illegal activity.

Why is interculturalism replacing the outmoded concepts of multiculturalism and assimilation?

An intercultural approach believes that the culture of the minority group is important and requires recognition and acceptance. An intercultural approach also requires that we focus attention and become aware of the accepted norms within the dominant culture. Key to the development of an intercultural approach is that attention is focused on the interaction between the dominant and minority ethnic communities. This invariably leads to a reflection on issues of how power is distributed in society and how decision-making is organised in society. The development of an intercultural approach implies the development of policy that promotes interaction, understanding and integration among and between different cultures and ethnic groups on the assumption that ethnic diversity can enrich society, without glossing over issues such as racism.

The concept of interculturalism has evolved over time and is now replacing earlier concepts such as policies based on assimilation, and increasingly interculturalism is replacing the concept of multiculturalism. The assimilationist approach viewed ethnic diversity as divisive and conflictual and tended to assume that minority groups were deficient, deprived and lacking in cultural capital. This approach promoted the absorption of minorities into the dominant culture in the belief that the socialisation of all into a shared value system was the only way forward; its aim was to make minority ethnic groups as invisible as possible.

The multicultural approach marked an important progression from the assimilationist approach and acknowledged the need for the recognition and celebration of different cultures and economic and social support for their integration into society. However, multiculturalism has been criticised for continuing to advocate that it was up to minorities to change and adapt in order to succeed, without any significant acknowledgement that racism exists and needs to be challenged through public policy. The emphasis of the multicultural approach is on the need for 'toleration' and 'better community relations' rather than acknowledging the need to change the negative attitudes and practices of the majority population.

The concept of interculturalism is increasingly being advocated by the European Commission in its policy statements and through specific programmes. Intercultural approaches are increasingly being applied to policy areas in Ireland, particularly in relation to education policy, and is one of the principles underpinning the recent White Paper on adult Education.

Notes

1   National Consultative Committee on Racism and Interculturalism.
    Progress Report 1998-2001, p17.
2   The National Co-ordinating Committee for the European Year
    Against Racism, Travellers in Ireland. 1998

PART TWO

THE CONTEXT

From Experience to Analysis

Migrants in Ireland
Tania Kaur McFarland

LIKE THE IRISH, we Indians are a very dispersed people and – also like the Irish – we have suffered from hardship and racism wherever we have settled. Many countries in the world have a significant Indian community, largely as a result of the direct or indirect effects of British colonial rule. For example, there are significant numbers of ethnic Indians living in South Africa, Kenya, the Middle East, the West Indies, Malaysia and of course the United Kingdom.

A more recent development in the movement of people has been the increased demand for highly trained Indian professionals, particularly in the information technology and medical fields.

A few words on my own background. I was born in Malaysia, to Sikh parents who settled there during the period of British rule. I was brought up and educated in Malaysia as a member of an Indian community that comprises approximately 15 per cent of the total population; it is essentially a multi-ethnic society.

In 1986 I married an Irishman and was immediately granted Irish citizenship. I then spent about eight years travelling and working in various countries, most of which have clearly defined policies towards the treatment of foreign workers and migrants. Some of these countries have vigorous and strict rules and regulations. I would acknowledge that some of the practices and enforcement of these practices make the current and proposed Irish and EU legislation indeed seem insipid in comparison.

I want to make the point that it is essential that there is a clear distinction between those migrants who are considered to be transient migrants, i.e. people who may be coming to study or work for a short time and have no initial plans to be considered for permanent residence, and those who arrive with the primary intention of seeking full citizenship. These I will refer to as 'stake-holders'.

My experience in the Middle Eastern countries is that there is a large group of non-nationals that is essential to the economy of the country. Members of this group are not given citizenship under any circumstances and may only be granted very limited rights and privileges. Some of these countries are largely dependent on foreign workers. This is not yet the situation in Ireland, but Ireland is now experiencing a significant need for additional people to fill the job vacancies. Obviously the state must have an efficient system for facilitating the short-term entry to the work force of many different ethnic people, while at the same time ensuring that there is an equitable and just system for helping those migrants who wish to become permanent residents (stake-holders).

In my experience, when people work abroad on a temporary basis they are often willing to tolerate an observance of local or state rules and regulations that would be considered draconian by nationals of any country (for example, re-entry and exit visas, work permits, restrictions on property purchase, etc). We should not forget that some migrants are here for essentially economic reasons, just as several of the middle-eastern countries are host to a large population of westerners. Ireland need not fear this development and should not be afraid of developing and implementing appropriate legislation in this regard. It goes without saying that such laws should be clearly seen as being fair and just.

On behalf of the Indian ethnic group who are currently working in Ireland, I have recently carried out a survey of a representative Indian group consisting of fifty people. These people are currently employed in the IT sector. Practical concerns expressed by these migrants that should be addressed are:

- *Re-entry Visa:* It is required of every non-EU migrant to obtain a re-entry visa before leaving Ireland for a visit abroad. It is very difficult to see what useful purpose this procedure serves. Non-EU migrants need a residential permit to stay in this country anyway and that can be entered into the passport. Would this not be sufficient for a returning migrant to prove his/her bona fides?
- *Residence Permit:* This is required on an annual basis, and is understandably used to monitor migrants living in the country. But in the Irish case it is required irrespective of the duration for which the migrant might have lived in this country. Even if one has lived here for the last twenty-five years he/she must have the Residence Permit. In some cases the Indians concerned have lived for a longer time in Ireland than they have lived in their own motherland! This is an area that should be further examined.
- *Visa for Spouse:* Recently we heard of many cases in which young men are employed here under contract. This contract may be for six months to two years. The employer would have the necessary work permit as well. For reasons unknown, when they ask for a visa for their spouse to join them, the Department refuses. The unfortunate perception is that what appear to be petty regulations come across as a type of institutionalised discrimination.

Due to the obvious sensitivities involved, of both the Irish people and migrants, it is vital that all issues under discussion should have a high degree of transparency and be subject to public debate. The average Indian migrant to Ireland is well educated, fluent in English and capable of contributing to the process of adaptation to a multi-ethnic society that is a part of Ireland now.

To summarise, I feel that we should have two objectives. First, the introduction and implementation of wide-ranging laws to prohibit any action or activity likely to create racial hatred or intolerance, and second, changes to our education system which would reflect the needs, both moral and material, of our changing society.

Both of these require a high degree of leadership by our elected representatives, journalists, educational bodies and the other state elements, e.g. An Garda Síochana, the Immigration Department, as well as the Churches and other socially active bodies.

One thing that I have found living in Ireland is that when some national crisis occurs there is a great tendency to look back and seek guidance from the past. Unfortunately, the world does not stand still and the past may not provide any useful ideas for moving forward. What we need now is a vision of what our society should be like in the future. It appears that the world is moving towards a high degree of racial and ethnic integration and Ireland cannot escape that reality. So let us look forward and grasp this opportunity for Ireland to show an example to the world by establishing the optimum conditions for harmony and tolerance.

TRAVELLERS AND RACISM
Martin Collins

The UN Global Conference on Racism in September 2001 in South Africa provides a good opportunity to focus on the experience of racism in Ireland and to learn from the experiences of other countries.

On a personal level, as a Traveller myself – one of Ireland's largest ethnic minorities – I am glad to have this opportunity to highlight the reality of racism as experienced by my own community.

We Travellers are a small, indigenous, ethnic minority who have been a part of Irish society for centuries. We have a long shared history, customs and traditions making us a group, recognised by ourselves and by the majority population as distinct. This distinctive identity and culture is based on a nomadic tradition, which sets us apart from the majority sedentary population.

Over the years, Travellers had to fight hard to resist a policy of assimilation and absorption, which was designed by the majority population without any input from Travellers or Traveller organisations.

We continue to be among the most marginalised and excluded communities within Irish society, and fare poorly on a wide range of indicators used to measure disadvantage, including poverty, social exclusion, health status, infant mortality, life expectancy, literacy, access to decision making and political representation, access to services, accommodation and living conditions.

These circumstances resulted in the Economic and Social Research Institute concluding, as far back as 1986, that 'the circumstances of the Irish Travelling people are intolerable, no humane and decent society once made aware of such circumstances could allow them to persist'. The situation today is as bad, if not worse.

More recently, 'Citizen Traveller', which is a government funded information and public awareness campaign, commissioned a major research project on the attitudes and feelings of the majority population towards the Traveller community. This research revealed:

- 42% of Irish people hold negative views towards Travellers
- 44% would not accept Travellers as members of their communities
- 93% would not accept a Traveller as part of his/her family
- 73% would not accept a Traveller as a friend.
- 40% of people would be annoyed at the possibility of an official halting site being established within two miles of their home while 75% of those with very unfavourable attitudes towards Travellers would be annoyed at the prospect.
- 3% or 80,000 Irish people have attempted to get Travellers to move on.

It revealed that almost half of the population is negatively disposed towards the Traveller community. Yet 65 per cent of Irish people have no contact with Travellers. These statistics vividly illustrate how much work remains to be done in confronting negative attitudes and prejudice towards our community.

Travellers share a nomadic tradition with Gypsies and Roma, and unfortunately, we also share a long history of persecution, rejection and social exclusion.

The Minority Rights Group Report, *Roma, Gypsies, a European Minority* (1985), says policies towards Roma and Gypsies have always consisted – in one form or another – of a negation of the people, their culture and their language. Past policies can be broadly grouped into three categories: exclusion, containment and assimilation.

I refer to these various reports to illustrate that there is a substantial body of evidence both at a national level and at an international level to support our claim that the experiences of Travellers, Roma and Gypsies throughout Europe is one of persecution and exclusion.

There's no doubt that Travellers have endured and are continuing to endure a long history of discrimination and exclusion on many levels, both at the institutionalised level and the individual level. Discrimination occurs when Travellers are refused access to public places or services such as shops, pubs, restaurants, laundrettes and so on. The most public manifestation of the anti-Traveller racism arises in the area of accommodation where you have the NIMBY (not in my back yard) syndrome.

At the institutional level, Travellers experience discrimination when services and policies are designed without regard to their potential to have a negative impact on Travellers. This can happen both intentionally and unintentionally. In our case, what this means is that services are designed by the majority population for the majority population. The Stephen Lawrence Inquiry, also known as the McPherson report, did offer in my view a very good definition of institutionalised racism. It is defined as:

> The collective failure of an organisation to provide an appropriate and professional service to people because of their colour, culture or ethnic origin. It can be seen or detected in processes, attitudes and behaviour which amount to discrimination through unwitting prejudice, ignorance, thoughtlessness and racist stereotyping which disadvantage minority ethnic people.

The strategy that emerges to address racism must recognise that racism does not just occur at the individual level but also at the institutional level. It's very convenient for us to imagine racism being perpetrated by groups of skinheads or extreme right wing groups without recognising the more subtle form of institutional racism. In my view, the most effective way to address institutional racism is to ensure that all decision-making processes and policy design and implementations are equality (including ethnicity) proofed. It's about placing equality considerations at the centre of decision-making and administrative procedures, in government departments and other organs of the state.

The media have an important role to play in combating racism. It has to be said that some sections of the media have been totally irresponsible when dealing with minority ethnic groups and the whole issue of racism. The Incitement to Hatred Act has a role to play in this regard and I am encouraged to hear that there is a commitment to review this legislation. While recognising the importance of free speech, this should not entitle anyone to incite hatred freely, particularly journalists and reporters who are in privileged positions, positions of power, and who sometimes use this platform to articulate what is in effect their own racism. We have to strike a balance between the right of free speech and the rights of ethnic minorities not to have their cultural integrity undermined or devalued.

To conclude, in addressing racism it is important that we include the form of racism experienced by Roma, Gypsies and Travellers. In doing this it should be recognised that Travellers, Roma, and Gypsies are not a homogenous group. Internal differences within the groups (gender, disability, sexual orientation, values, etc.) must be acknowledged and addressed. The role of independent, non-governmental organisations to give voice to the experience of ethnic groups must be acknowledged. Three types of strategy need to be put in place to address racism. Firstly, an education and public awareness campaign, which has a role to play in informing people and in trying to challenge and change attitudes. Secondly, there is the whole area of legislation; unless we have strong, effective legislation I don't think people's behaviour will change. Thirdly and finally, I think what we really need to challenge is the whole ideology that underpins racism. This ideology encompasses a set of beliefs and values, which suggest that white, settled society is superior and that Travellers and other ethnic groups are inherently inferior.

REFUGEES AND ASYLUM-SEEKERS
Dr Jean Pierre Eyanga

What do we mean by racism? Where does it come from? How does it manifest itself? Who are the authors? Why racism and xenophobia? Is there any way to tackle the plague of racism? I will try to answer these questions in respect of refugees and asylum-seekers here in Ireland. It will not be an academic exercise but rather a practical and realistic one.

Racism and xenophobia are prevalent in each country on planet earth. That's why conferences and meetings are organised throughout the world on the issue. However, the most important question for us is: do Irish people and the government really want to tackle racism and xenophobia? Tangible actions are necessary.

In Ireland we have been victims of two forms of racism: the active form and the passive form. The active form is experienced mainly through verbal and physical assault. The passive form is mainly practised by institutions and so-called 'clever people' who, in doing nothing to stop racists, allow others to act and react badly to people of different skin colour or cultures. This form is not as easy to identify.

Examples of racist incidents that I and other colleagues have heard include in one school, a young girl being assaulted for months by an Irish boy from the same school because she was black. The principal was informed of this but he never stopped the boy. One day, when the girl was doing sport, all her clothes were put into the toilet bowl so she couldn't put them on. The only reaction the principal had was to say 'I am sorry', but he never punished the boy.

A further example is something that happened to me. I was in an area in Dublin one evening when I was kicked by a group of young children. I also received hate mail calling me a 'nigger', a 'bogus refugee', etc. I lodged a complaint with the Gardaí. They asked me why I chose that area. 'We cannot control those people,' they said. I never received a reply to my complaint. Finally, my only solution was to leave the area, as I realised that I was not properly protected. If five-year olds can act in this manner, what might the parents and other adults do?

In another example, a refugee was on a bus. Somebody entered the bus and started to assault him verbally. He stayed quiet while the abuser strongly mocked him. The victim asked the driver not to open the door and to call the Gardaí. The driver called the Gardaí but opened the door to let the abuser go. The most shocking thing is that none of the ten or twelve people present reacted to the assault and none of them wanted to confirm the attack when Gardaí interviewed them.

Accommodation is the area where racism and xenophobia are a daily experience for many refugees and asylum-seekers. When making a phone call to landlords and landladies, because of the names and foreign accents the answer is nearly always the same: 'It's gone', 'We are full up', even if the place is still available.

So we can say that refugees and asylum-seekers face racism and xenophobia every day and almost everywhere, from professional services, in gaining access to a job, in social welfare, in education, in training, in accommodation, in the participation in common cultural, social and political activities.

To tackle racism and xenophobia in Ireland a few conditions must be fulfilled. The first one is that all the decision and policy makers of the government, political parties, trade unions, Churches and all major institutions should make a clear and strong statement expressing their real will for and commitment to the elimination of all forms of discrimination, especially racism and xenophobia from Ireland. This would be the most important step of this battle.

The second condition, which the Irish government has recently met, is the ratification of the international UN Convention on the Elimination of all Forms of Racism.

The recruitment and incorporation of members of ethnic minorities in state administration professions such as Gardaí, civil servants, teachers, etc., would make a sustainable contribution to addressing the problem.

The Irish people and their institutions should look at the different layers in the causes and manifestation of racism in Ireland. Refugees and asylum-seekers will play their part in this endeavour.

BLACK AND IRISH
Rose Tuelo Brock

It appears that Ireland has been dragged kicking and screaming towards ratifying the UN Convention on the Elimination of All

Forms of Racism. This has involved putting into place legislation on equality and anti-racism. However, there is still a lot of work to be done.

The public, the Gardaí, the teachers, and the politicians themselves need to be educated and familiarised with the details of the legislation and the expectations and hopes of what the legislation is supposed to achieve.

This is essential because, out there, on the streets, young black men still get beaten, some report experiencing harassment from individual members of the Garda Síochana, black women still experience verbal abuse, foreigners get abused both verbally and physically, while politicians continue to use terms such as 'bogus', 'floods', and 'hordes' in regard to asylum-seekers.

The new equality legislation is to be welcomed. There is a real danger, however, that victims of racism may feel inhibited from taking any action under the legislation. There is a need for education and training of teachers, civil servants and members of the Gardaí, for example, in not only understanding the legislation but also in being encouraged to put it into practice.

Legislation should be more proactive than reactive. The introduction of re-entry visas for every visit outside the country, no matter how short, to people who already have valid residents' permits, is one such piece of legislation. Inviting workers from different parts of the world to come but restricting the entry of even their spouses, is, in my mind, a recipe for breaking up families. Is this what such legislation is intended for?

Whilst I am very much encouraged by the formation of the new Garda Intercultural Unit and related initiatives, there is still a great need for education and workshops on racism and anti-racism in the Gardaí and other public services. We all need to examine our own views and question our beliefs and prejudices and open ourselves to learning skills of treating other people, different from us, with respect, affirmation and acceptance.

I think that there is an opportunity for the school system to take anti-racism on board. This can be started from early on in the school. When I arrived in this country some twenty-one years ago, I was shocked and demeaned by what I call 'The Black Baby Syndrome'. It seemed to me as if the children looked at me as the black baby for whom they had had to give up their pennies. Today, as I walk around, I am still not sure if the children do not still think like that.

In the early years, at school and in the home and through children's television programmes, it is important to see pictures of children from different parts of the world and to learn about their different ways of life. This can be a way of introducing young children to difference and encouraging them to associate difference with acceptance and affirmation, rather than derision.

It is important also that young children learn that the fact that people are different does not mean that they are stupid or threatening. They should be given the opportunity to see people in different parts of the world acting as teachers, nurses, doctors as well as labourers, and not always as victims.

In secondary schools, special courses can be introduced through the civic classes and during transition year that might go some way towards explaining phenomena such as regional wars, the need to flee, and why some states remain poor even when they have rich natural resources. The role of developed countries and multi-nationals should be included in such studies.

Often people are encouraged to be tolerant of black people or those from other cultures. I have a problem with the words 'tolerate' and 'tolerant'. For me the words smack of negativity. In my opinion, when you tolerate something, it is because you are uncomfortable with it, uneasy and threatened. People who are of a different colour are human and no different. They might look different and have some different cultural practices, some of which we might find peculiar, but being black is not an aberration. We are like this because of a concentration of melanin, which we all have except that mine is different to yours. This melanin is only in our skin, and does not exist in our brain. I am normal and have dignity and integrity, and therefore I do not want to be tolerated. I want to be *affirmed* and *accepted*, because *I have the right to be*.

There is a tendency for selective reporting of issues to do with members of ethnic groups, which gives the negative characters and happenings while glossing over positive facts. The media should take care with the language used. Derogatory, defamatory terms ought to be shunned in talking or writing about particular groups; and generalising characteristics, especially negative characteristics, should be avoided. Let us always keep in mind that corruption, greed and dishonesty are human failings and not those of a particular group of people; that criminals and cheats are in all parts of the world and all walks of life.

The way that the Third World is presented in the media also has implications for minority ethnic groups in Ireland. If the Third World is represented or referred to in a consistently derogatory way, then this will have implications for how black people and others from minority ethnic groups will be perceived in Ireland.

We ought to have representatives of different communities working in the media. By now, there should be more, for example, black or Asian reporters, programme-presenters and actors in RTÉ as well as in the newspapers. It would be encouraging to see the media giving opportunities to members of minority ethnic groups to take an active part in reporting, writing, and discussion programmes. Let us bear in mind that people in these groups have mouths and minds and do not need always to be talked about and on behalf of, when they are capable of doing so themselves. The 'does he take sugar' mentality ought to disappear. It is so demeaning, so disrespectful, that it always perplexes me that it is still such a common practice in this day and age. You see it every day, everywhere. If you are in a campaign about debt cancellation or some such campaign, the photos of celebrities or well-known members of the Church or some such people will be the ones whose utterances and pictures will appear in the newspaper. Very few of the ordinary people are interviewed, even if they are so willing and active and always there.

To conclude, let me emphasise this: *there are black people who are Irish and there are Irish people who are black.* They are not all footballers or actors. There are many who are normal, everyday people with their own various talents and abilities. It is high time that the politicians and the public became aware and acknowledged this. Black people should not always have to explain their Irishness.

Immigration Policy in Ireland

Piaras Mac Éinrí

Introduction

IRELAND IS traditionally a country of strong emigration. This has changed in the very recent past, as the Celtic Tiger economy takes off and more and more immigrants are needed to work here. At the same time, the country is also attracting increasing numbers of asylum-seekers and refugees.

These changes raise the issue of what kind of society Ireland wants to become. What would multiculturalism, Irish-style, be like in practice? What policy, legislative and practical changes need to be made in a country with little historical experience of diversity? How does one become Irish?

In the meantime, in the absence of clear political directives, the issue of racism inevitably arises. Tough legislation is now in place, but one must ask (a) whether effective enforcement mechanisms will be put in place and (b) whether legislation alone can provide a route to change and to the acceptance of a multicultural society.

At the same time, moves are afoot to promote a more pluralist and diverse society, but largely through voluntarist means. Will this be enough? What models and mechanisms can be found in other places?

IMMIGRATION AND ECONOMIC DEVELOPMENT

The modernisation of the country

Until the recent past, Ireland was a country of emigration. From the Great Famine of the 1840s to the 1950s, the natural increase in the population was continually offset by out-migration on a scale that was relatively higher than any other European country, leading to an almost continuous decline in the population for more than a century (Chart 1, see p.80).

The adoption at the end of the 1950s of new economic policies[1] based on the encouragement of foreign direct investment (FDI) from the multinational corporate sector led to a turnaround in the decade which followed, with increased job creation, a dramatic drop in out-migration and a consequent rise in the marriage rate.

Ireland's adherence to the European Community in 1973 even led to net in-migration, for the first time in modern history, although this was largely explained by the return of experienced Irish migrants, usually with families, to meet specific skills shortages in the Irish economy (Chart 2, see p.80).

Emigration slowed down but did not cease and immigration by non-Irish persons remained relatively insignificant. With the increase in the marriage rate in the 1960s, the population grew by almost 22 per cent between 1961 and 1981 (Chart 3, see p.81).

In the 1980s, the painful effects of the post-EC re-structuring of much traditional Irish industry (used to a protectionist environment and lacking economies of scale), combined with unwise economic management, led to a substantial loss of jobs, at the very time when the baby-boom generation of the 1960s was emerging onto the job market. The consequence was a dramatic rise in unemployment and an even more dramatic return to high emigration rates. In 1988-

89 alone, 70,600 persons, or approximately 2 per cent of the
population, left (Chart 4, see p.81).

The 1990s – a period of dramatic change

The 1990s saw the emergence of a very different Ireland. The
introduction of a largely successful policy of peaceful
industrial relations and joint wage bargaining through a
mechanism involving all of the social partners, based in part
on the German model, was a key feature. The major
investment in education that the State had made in the 1970s
and 1980s began to pay off in ever-greater numbers of well-
educated workers. Fiscal and other investment incentives (in
particular, zero, and later very low, export taxes) made Ireland
a very attractive location within the European Union,
especially for such sectors as IT and pharmaceuticals, and led
to a major increase in foreign direct investment. Tight
government fiscal and monetary policy, partly in preparation
for entry into the euro, kept inflation low. While it has been
argued that workers paid the highest price as the burden of
taxation shifted from the corporate sector to the individual
employee, there can be no doubting that the results were
impressive.

The 'Celtic Tiger' boom that has characterised Ireland from
the mid-1990s is not a chimera. Real growth rates in the late
1990s, at more than 8 per cent of GDP, were the highest in the
OECD area; indeed they exceeded any other member State by
a factor of more than two. Moreover, the economic boom did
generate new jobs. In the decade 1991–2000, almost half a
million new jobs were added to the Irish economy, an
expansion of 43 per cent in the total labour force (Chart 5, see
p.82). To quote the International Labour Organisation:

> Since 1993 the Irish economy has expanded very rapidly,
> with annual rates of growth in excess of 8 per cent

averaged over the 1993–1997 period. Total employment grew by 25 per cent between 1993–1998 and unemployment fell to less than 12 per cent in 1997. By 1998 the standardised unemployment rate had fallen to less than 8 per cent – below the EU average. Continued growth is forecast in the medium term.[2]

The Irish Department of Finance, in its National Development Plan for 2000–2006 is similarly upbeat in its comments on the years 1994–1999

Ireland's economic progress in recent years has exceeded the targets set in the last NDP by a wide margin. GNP growth averaged about 7.5 per cent per annum in real terms. This was much higher than the 3.5 per cent annual GNP growth envisaged in the 1994–99 National Development Plan.

One of the most encouraging aspects of Ireland's economic performance over this period is that unlike earlier periods of expansion, output growth was extremely employment-intensive. The numbers at work grew by over 370,000. While the labour force grew strongly, the unemployment rate fell from over 15 per cent in 1993 to about 6 per cent in early 1999.

These employment targets were easily surpassed with employment growing by about 370,000 in the last five years, an annual average increase of about 5 per cent. On an International Labour Organisation (ILO) basis, unemployment has fallen by about 125,000 since 1993. As a result the unemployment rate is now about 6 per cent – well below the EU average. Long term unemployment has also fallen dramatically, and now represents less than 3 per cent of the work force.

This progress was achieved against a background of very strong labour force growth. Positive demographic factors, increased labour force participation – particularly by women – and net immigration have enabled the labour force to grow rapidly. Over the period of the Plan the work force grew by over 250,000. The population boom of the 1970s resulted in an increasing young work force in the 1990s. Moreover, as a result of enhanced investment in education and training over the last twenty years the new cohorts of entrants to the labour force were more highly educated than their predecessors. As a result, the work force was well suited to respond to the needs of the expanding manufacturing and services sectors.[3]

The latest bulletin of the Department of Finance (March 2001) indicates that unemployment is now at 3.9 per cent. The Department of Finance estimates that GDP grew by 10.7 per cent in 2000 while GNP grew by 8.6 per cent. For 2001, it estimates that GDP will grow by 8.8 per cent while GNP will grow by 7.4 per cent.[4] While problems of social exclusion, literacy, and poor education and training still exist, there is no longer a substantial reserve of unemployed persons waiting to enter the labour market.

There is no reason to foresee a major downturn in projected economic and employment indicators in the short to medium term. One note of caution to be sounded concerns the state of the US economy. A serious downturn would have multiple consequences for Ireland as US investment would slow down, new projects would be placed on hold and export growth would suffer.

Economic growth and the labour force

Four traditional sources of additional workers in an expanding economy may be identified: (a) untapped reserves, especially women outside the paid labour force (b) the unemployed, especially the long-term unemployed (c) the natural increase in the age cohort of the population entering the labour force (d) immigrants, including returning Irish migrants.

Ireland traditionally had a low level of female participation in the paid labour force. This was reinforced by societal attitudes and even offical policy until the relatively recent past.[5] In the past ten years, however, there has been a considerable change; Ireland now finds itself in the mid-range of EU member States with almost half of all adult women in the paid labour force (CSO Quarterly National Household Survey, Fourth Quarter 2000).

It should be noted that the Irish situation is very different from that of Italy, as Ireland still has a relatively young population. Nevertheless, the underlying demographic reality has undergone a significant shift. Irish demography might fairly have been described as unique by European standards until the fairly recent past. Arguably, the country could not have been said to have completed the classic European demographic transition until after the 1960s. In recent decades, however, and notably since the 1980s, there has been a rapid fall in Irish fertility rates (Chart 6, see p.82). While these have not converged totally with the EU average (Chart 7, see p.83), and there is even some evidence of a modest upturn in recent years, total fertility rates (TFR) seem to be stabilising at a rate slightly below the population replacement level.

Even if one allows for fluctuations, it is hardly likely that the high fertility rates, which were the traditional norm, will recur. In practical terms, the very rapid growth in the school and college-level population in the 1980s, itself a result of the changes in the 1960s already referred to, has been succeeded by a much more modest pattern of growth. The population of school-leaving age will in fact peak in the next ten years.

This leaves immigration. Immigration flows into Ireland could historically be classified in fairly predictable ways: (a) return Irish migration, although never on the scale found in Mediterranean countries such as Italy (b) high-skills immigration, usually non-permanent, within the multinational sector (c) 'counter-cultural' immigration from Britain and continental EU states (d) retirees, especially from the UK. It should be noted that apart from (b) and (c) – where the presence of a modest number of countercultural immigrants was disproportionately influential because of their preference for settlement in rural areas – few immigrants came to Ireland before the mid-1990s who were not either of Irish background or British. Non-EU immigration, the multinational sector aside, was insignificant (Chart 8, see p.83).

New immigration flows

It is in the light of the above that the very dramatic changes in the past five years must be appreciated. A few comments about statistical data might be in order first. The only sources of data easily available are from the Central Statistics Office. While the Census does give a reasonably accurate picture, the most recent figures date from 1996, when the country was only on the threshold of change. Intercensal data are derived through extrapolations from the Quarterly National Household Survey (QNHS) and a number of other sources, but this is not an exact science and the QNHS sample size is not sufficient to enable more than very broad generalisations to be made (see further reservations below). Immigration-related data from immigration and police authorities, social welfare or other sources is not easily available and Irish monitoring of immigrant residents is relaxed. Aggregate figures in intercensal periods for 'Irish', 'UK', 'Rest of EU', 'USA' and 'Rest of World' categories must also be treated with some caution, as the 'foreign-born' will inevitably include a percentage who are in fact the foreign-born children of returning Irish migrants. While it is impossible to estimate these figures (the next Census will enable a clearer picture to be established) it seems safe to predict that Irish-born returned migrants and their children constitute a falling proportion of in-migrants as a whole. This is because the volume of Irish out-migrants itself fell in the early 1990s, leaving a decreasing number of recent Irish emigrants in the crucial 25-34 age cohort where the propensity to return (usually for family reasons, to bring up one's children in Ireland) may be supposed to be strongest.

What is not in dispute (Chart 9, see p.84) is the scale of the overall inward migratory flows. In the period 1995–2000, approximately a quarter of a million persons migrated to Ireland, of whom about half were returning Irish (but see the comments above, which would suggest the real figure for Irish, if we include children born to Irish parent(s), must be higher). The aggregate figure for immigrants in this five-year period is an astonishing 7 per cent approximately of the 1996 population (3.6 million). There are no parallels to these figures in other EU countries. This figure of 7 per cent for in-migration in 1995–2000 would be the equivalent of close to 4 million persons in France. Moreover, this situation of substantial net immigration is set to continue for several years to come, although the actual figures will clearly be influenced by international and internal economic developments.

It will be evident that the great majority of immigrants are returned Irish migrants or come from other EU member States or the USA. The CSO's *Population and Migration* estimates up to April 2000, published in September 2000, indicate that only 12 per cent or 29,400 over the five years came from outside the EU and the USA.[6]

Although this figure may appear small it is not neglible; moreover there has been a sharp upward trend since 1999. It is also possible that a degree of intercensal undercounting is taking place and that the sampling methods underlying the Quarterly National Household Survey (QNHS) do not enable an accurate figure for total immigration to be extrapolated. The CSO's own document alludes to this difficulty in pointing out that they are based on the

> QNHS which covers private households only. Because of recent increases in the number of asylum-seekers who are accommodated in institutions such as hotels and hostels, the classification of immigrants by country of origin and nationality for more recent years may be subject to a wider margin of error than the other estimates in this release.[7]

At the very least this would suggest that more focused statistical methods are needed. In the meantime, we must await the results of the forthcoming Census (delayed due to the foot and mouth scare) for an accurate picture of the true current population and the real number of immigrants.

Subject to the caveat entered above, Chart 10 (p.84) shows the year by year change in in-migration between 1995 and 2000 and Chart 11 (p.85) shows the regions of origin.

In a general sense, and in distinction to Italy in particular, Ireland has not yet become a major pole of attraction for non-EU migrants. However, there is a rising trend of non-EU migration, both short- and long-term.

Before considering the policy responses to the changes in immigration, one may distinguish the following main types of immigration flows:

- return Irish migration
- in-migration from other EU and EEA (European Economic Area) countries
- asylum-seekers
- programme refugees
- high-skills in-migration from non-EEA countries
- other in-migration from non-EEA countries

The first two categories do not require, in the strict sense, an immigration policy at all, as the persons concerned have a more or less absolute legal right to live and work in Ireland, a right guaranteed by the Irish Constitution in the case of Irish citizens, by the 1951 Common Travel Area Agreement (and later the Treaty of Rome and other legal instruments) in the case of British citizens, and by the Treaties of Rome and Maastricht and other legal arrangements in the case of the citizens of other EU and/or EEA member States.

It should be noted in all cases, however, that immigration should not be confused with integration, whether the latter is interpreted within an assimilationist or multicultural context. The absence of a proper framework for the reception and integration of all non-Irish workers in the Irish labour economy may be a topic that is somewhat beyond the scope of this brief paper, but the least that can be said is that it can lead to considerable difficulties for individual migrants and, unless tackled, can only perpetuate a variety of hidden, implicit and explicit forms of exclusion of and/or discrimination against such individuals. The tough new legislation against discrimination which is now in place and which (correctly) does not distinguish between EU and non-EU migrants, may provide a way forward, but it remains to be seen what case law, policy and practice will emerge.

The third category, asylum-seekers, is also only partly a labour-related issue. This is because asylum-seekers apply to stay under the terms of the 1951 UN Refugee Convention. Pending a decision in his/her case, an asylum-seeker does not have the right to work in Ireland. There was a 'one-off' decision to allow such a right, on 26 July 1999, to asylum-seekers who could demonstrate that that had been in the country for at least a year before that date, but this decision was not rolled over the following year and the Department of Justice, Equality and Law Reform has stated that it will not be repeated. The vast majority of asylum cases are rejected.

Nonetheless, the topic of asylum-seekers (Chart 12, see p.85) should not be omitted for a variety of reasons. First, although asylum-seekers probably constitute no more than 10 per cent of all foreign immigrants to Ireland since 1995, they have been the subject of considerable media coverage, some of it negative. Secondly, asylum-seekers who have acquired refugee status, or humanitarian leave to remain, then become eligible to enter the regular labour market, raising all the usual issues about training, education, discrimination and so on. Thirdly, the absence of an American-style quota-based immigration policy, or indeed of any kind of transparent immigration policy, has meant that, in practice, some proportion of asylum-seekers arriving in Ireland would more correctly be described as economic migrants, not in itself a term of opprobrium although it is sometimes used as such. Fourthly, there is strong anecdotal evidence that many asylum-seekers are working in the black market anyway – Ireland has considerable labour shortages both in high- and low-skills positions. Finally, asylum-seekers are strongly concentrated in urban areas, in spite of Government action since April 2000 to disperse more recent arrivals outside of Dublin. Ethnically-based organisations of asylum-seekers constitute what for Ireland is a new phenomenon: how to deal with the organised ethnicity of the 'other' within Irish social space. Although asylum-seekers are small in number, they do represent the cutting edge of social innovation in the construction of new identities that contest the traditional, implicitly assimilationist, model.

'Programme Refugees' constitute a special case unconnected with the needs of the labour market. As with other EU member states, they come to Ireland as a result of a Government decision, usually in consultation with EU partners, to waive the usual requirement for the individual to bring a case at law to become a 'Convention Refugee' under the terms of the 1951 Convention in favour of an organised quota-based system providing for a specific number of refugees from a particular conflict situation to be admitted without the burden of individual proof having to be established before the courts. Thus, Bosnian and Kosovar programme refugees, once admitted, are effectively given the same access and rights to training, education and employment as EU citizens, although initially they were only allowed to stay for a limited duration. This does not mean that there are not problems – the tendency of the State in Ireland to rely on self-help and voluntary organisations rather than statutory provision is an issue, while the earlier experience of the Vietnamese was disastrous, as a policy of 'dispersal' was implemented without support structures and merely led to a drift back to Dublin.

The two remaining categories to be considered (and the only ones where it has been necessary to give consideration to a strictly labour-market oriented immigration policy) are thus high-skills in-migration from non-EU countries and other in-migration from non-EU countries. This paper will consider the various measures put in place by the Government to encourage specific categories of high-skills workers from outside the EU, while contrasting these policies with the increasingly widespread implementation of a Gastarbeiter-type short-term work visa programme for low-skills workers. In 2000 a total of 18,006 short term work visas were issued (Chart 13, see p.86) to nationals of more than 120 countries, marking a considerable increase over previous years. This figure is set to increase further, to a probable 25,000–30,000 for 2018. Catering and service industry positions accounted for the largest numbers (Chart 14, see p.86) while workers from Central or Eastern Europe were most strongly represented (Chart 15, see p.87).

THE REGULATORY SYSTEM

The institutional framework

Historically, Ireland has not, as noted, received any significant immigration flows. As a relatively poor, peripheral European country with strong and sustained emigration, limited employment opportunities and no traditional colonial ties to majority world countries (unlike several other EU member states), little consideration was given to a formal immigration policy. As has been documented elsewhere[9], the prevailing official attitude towards foreign immigrants (the legal term 'alien' was generally employed) was one of caution, if not outright opposition.

The above notwithstanding, small communities, notably Italian and Chinese, have been established in Ireland for several decades. Ireland's Jewish community, most of whom arrived toward the end of the 19th century, have played a role in Irish public life out of all proportion to their numbers.[10] While they are not an immigrant community, mention should also be made of the Traveller community, an indigenous nomadic group whose lifestyle can in a number of respects be compared to that of Roma and Sinti in other parts of Europe.

In examining official and popular discourses, two strands may be discerned – exclusion, whether outright or through a policy of social containment – and forced assimilation. Thus, members of the Traveller community were subjected in the 1960s to an official policy of forced resettlement, on the one hand, while experiencing exclusion and even persecution at the popular level, on the other.

In an overwhelmingly mono-cultural Roman Catholic country with few minorities and an insignificant number of foreign-born residents not of Irish extraction, the prevailing attitude was probably less one of deliberate outright rejection or exclusion than an informally codified value system whereby those who were different 'knew their place'. Moreover, there was no part of Ireland (with the partial exception of two areas of Dublin where many of the city's Jews lived) where the presence of minorities or immigrants was publicly and visibly manifest through an identifiable immigrant quarter.

It is in this light, therefore, that the recent changes should be interpreted. Although there had been some previous cases, all of them refugees (Hungarians in 1956; Chileans in 1973; Vietnamese in 1979; Iranian Baha'i in the mid-1980s and Bosnians in the early 1990s) substantial non-Irish immigration is very recent indeed, arising only from the mid-1990s onwards. As pointed out previously, there was also a rise in the number of asylum-seekers in the same, later, period.

Ireland thus experienced, within a short space of time, a substantial rise in non-Irish immigration, mostly from other EU countries, and a smaller but significant rise in non-EU immigrants, whether asylum-seekers, illegal immigrants or immigrant workers on short-term work permits. The country has thus been faced with the difficulties of constructing immigration and integration policies against a background of a rapidly changing picture, limited experience, a less than positive attitude towards difference and a largely mono-cultural tradition. Apart from the rather ad-hoc arrangements made until the recent past for asylum-seekers and refugees, and the more formal arrangements now in place for the same community (although still heavily reliant on the voluntary sector) it would be fair to say that there was little that could be described as an 'official planning process' on immigration.

Legal/regulatory framework

The Department of Justice, Equality and Law Reform (formerly the Department of Justice) is responsible for immigration law and immigration controls in Ireland. That Department is also primarily responsible for the Irish contribution to developing EU and international policy on immigration and related issues.

Other Departments also have a role to play. The Department of Enterprise, Trade and Employment (the relevant part of which was formerly the Department of Labour) is responsible for the issuing of work permits. The Department of Foreign Affairs is responsible for certain operational aspects of the Ireland's immigration and visa regulations outside the country, although the Department of Justice, Equality and Law Reform retains primary responsibility. However, in one specific field, that of programme refugees (e.g. the Bosnian and Kosovar Albanian communities) the Department of Foreign Affairs has been involved in a key capacity.

Recent changes to legislation, policy and practice have included a greater degree of inter-departmental cooperation in the fields of immigration and integration.[11] Moreover, insofar as a public debate has taken place at all and changes have been put in train, the situation of refugees and asylum-seekers, while unrelated in the strict sense to immigration and the labour market, has been the main impetus for change and the most visible example of changing forward thinking at official level, although the new work visa arrangements (more below) also represent an important labour market initiative.

As a general rule it may still be said that the Department of Justice, Equality and Law Reform retains primary and usually sole responsibility for all core aspects of Ireland's immigration policy, including admission, residence and citizenship issues.

IMMIGRATION AND THE LABOUR MARKET

Regulations governing the entry of foreigners into Ireland
The most significant legislation governing the admission of foreigners into Ireland was the Aliens Act 1935. In this Act the word 'alien' meant a person who was not a citizen of *Saorstát Eireann* (the Irish Free State, forerunner to the present state of Ireland). Rooted as it was in earlier wartime (World War 1) British legislation, the scope of the Act was extremely wide-ranging and conferred sweeping executive powers on the Minister for Justice. The Minister had the right to forbid landing or entry into the State by any alien, to impose various restrictions on such persons as he saw fit, to forbid them leaving, to deport them, to require them to live in particular districts or places, to prohibit them from living in particular districts or places, and to require them to comply with particular provisions such as registration, change of address, travel, employment and other matters. The Minister had power to use the police, military and customs and excise to give effect to these regulations, to determine the nationality to be ascribed to aliens whose nationality was unknown or uncertain and to require hotelkeepers and similar persons to keep records. In all cases the onus of proof in the event of any contestation lay on the alien or alleged alien. The Minister did not have to give reasons for his decisions and there was no appeal.

The Aliens Order 1946 further codified these draconian provisions with a range of additional specific provisions. The powers given to police and other authorities were extended further, including the power given to immigration and police authorities to arrest a person without warrant if he/she was 'reasonably suspected' of having acted or being about to act in contravention of the Order.

Since that time various measures have been introduced that defined new rights for certain classes of people wishing to come to Ireland. Thus, shared membership of the British Commonwealth, which ended on 1 January 1949 when Ireland declared a Republic and left the Commonwealth, and which allowed for freedom of travel, residence and work for Irish people in Britain (similar rights were accorded to British citizens in Ireland), was replaced within a few years by the Common Travel Area Agreement, which effectively reinstated the same rights even though no formal constitutional relationship existed any longer between the two jurisdictions and removed passport controls of citizens of the two jurisdictions. At the same time, close cooperation between the Irish and UK immigration authorities continued and deepened over the years. This effectively meant that, while Irish and British citizens were free to live, work, and vote (except in Presidential elections in Ireland and in referenda) in one another's countries, there was also close cooperation and coordination of the immigration and visa policies applied to would-be visitors from third-country states.

Such cooperation continues today. This largely explains why Ireland and Britain have jointly stayed out of the most of the arrangements put in place after Schengen. For Ireland to have gone in while Britain stayed out would have raised extremely complex and probably insuperable issues for the control of the movement of persons between the two jurisdictions. One should also distinguish between the application of common visa regimes for visitors, where a common Anglo-Irish approach has largely given way to EU-wide cooperation, and the application of policies to control permanent immigration into Ireland, where the country has traditionally followed a highly restrictive approach.

The 1956 Irish Nationality and Citizenship Act (modified in 1986) codified rights to Irish citizenship through birth, descent and naturalisation, including the right to citizenship through an Irish grandparent. The Act created a general although discretionary eligibility for citizenship through naturalisation after a period of five years (with the exception of naturalisation through marriage, for which a separate regime applied). With Ireland's membership of the European Community (later European Union) on 1 January 1973 came the right of freedom of movement of workers and, more recently (the Treaty of Maastricht 1993), the right of freedom of movement of all citizens of the European Union. Moreover, all citizens of EEA (European Economic Area) countries, which apart from EU member states also includes Liechtenstein, Iceland and Norway, have had essentially similar rights since 1992.

In sum, therefore, one may distinguish two important and entirely divergent trends.

On the one hand, a series of specific measures opened up the possibility of immigration to certain categories of foreign-born persons – those deemed to be entitled to Irish citizenship, British citizens, citizens of other EU member states and citizens of EEA states. These persons all have the right to work in Ireland and no work permit is required.

On the other hand, Ireland had no traditional 'mother-country' ties to former colonies. No other immigration route into Ireland exists except for naturalisation, asylum, a limited work permit regime – see below – and certain exceptional individual decisions made from time to time by the Minister of the day. The latter category included the introduction in the 1980s of a controversial 'passports for sale' policy for wealthy investors, since discontinued following various political controversies concerning payments for passports. In general, until the recent past, the economic climate in Ireland was not conducive to immigration.

In the case of naturalisation through marriage, it is instructive to note that the husbands of Irish citizens could only apply after being married for a period of some years (thus initially preventing them from competing for jobs in a market of scarce opportunities) whereas foreign wives were given automatic and immediate citizenship (on the presumption that women would not enter the paid labour force in any event). This distinction was successfully legally challenged in the 1980s and led to the 1986 amendment already referred to, which applied a less liberal rather than a more liberal one to both sexes. The lesson one may draw is that official attitudes were largely influenced by labour market considerations.

In practice, therefore, the earlier, draconian legislation referred to above has remained in place for most non-EU would-be immigrants. With the exception of the admission of middle and senior management from the multinational sector, it would be fair to say that until the very recent past the mindset, policies and practices of immigration officials in Ireland in respect of putative non-EU immigrants had probably changed little since the 1930s.

Some evidence of these general attitudes may be found in the almost complete absence of integration (as opposed to immigration) policies until the 1990s and in the arbitrary practices of the 1980s when asylum-seekers were sometimes bundled back onto aircraft or even imprisoned, often on such flimsy pretexts as the assertion that they had not used some particular form of words in making their claim. A general suspicion of foreigners, unless they were white and/or wealthy, was characteristic of the attitude of the Department of Justice. This was most clearly in evidence in the operation of visa policies for visitors (i.e. where permanent residence was not even being sought) where arbitrary decisions were frequent, no explanation was given and no appeal was allowed.

Finally, while the legislation was not updated, and in certain respects has yet to be, a considerable body of codified policy and practice did inevitably develop. Unfortunately, as this was not embodied in legislation and was thus not generally open to parliamentary or public scrutiny, it perpetuated the general climate of secrecy and non-accountability that had come to be typical of the Department of Justice.

The presence and role of immigrants in the labour market
Ireland's position after World War 2 was different from that of any other northern European country, although clearly not different from that which obtained in southern Europe, including Italy and Spain. Large numbers of Irish emigrants, as has already been seen, continued to find work in Britain and other countries. As a largely rural country with little industrialisation and no way of absorbing large numbers of indigenous workers, the question of bilateral country-to-country regimes and of immigrant quotas simply did not arise for Ireland. Insofar as immigrants were admitted to Ireland to undertake specialist work in the public or private sector, the over-riding principle in the issuing of work permits was the need for the potential employer to demonstrate that no Irish citizen (after 1973 this was extended to include other EU and later EEA citizens) was available to do the work in question.

It would thus be fair in a general sense to describe Ireland as a non-immigrant country apart from certain exceptions (such as employees in transnational corporations) where access to the labour market was determined on a case by case basis by negotiation between employer, the Department of Labour and the would-be immigrant. Numbers, as has been shown in section 1, were small before the 1990s.

Within its limits this regime could be both flexible, relatively speedy and efficient and even liberal. Thus, within the university sector, the notion that an Irish or EEA person might not be available to do the work was often interpreted generously – after all, every academic position is unique and a statement from a university that a particular individual was needed to take up a particular post was not usually questioned.

There were, however, a number of obvious drawbacks to this ad hoc, market-driven regime. The most obvious are that the work permit rather than work visa regime effectively tied the immigrant to a particular employer, while the lack of clarity and transparency regarding family reunification rights – an issue which has yet to be fully clarified – sometimes meant that immigrants who were granted work permits had difficulties in having members of their immediate families admitted to join them.

It would be fair to say that all of these issues affected a relatively small number of individuals before the late 1990s.

New policies
Irish policy, for reasons already explained, has developed in a rather piecemeal way over several decades. The country does not have a formal quota-based immigration policy with country quotas or (with certain exceptions) special category immigration visas. In effect, the admission of immigrants has been largely market-led, as the onus has been firmly placed on employers to show that a particular individual or group of

individuals was required and that no EEA persons were available and willing to do the job.

It is this market-led, administratively light policy which is now proving inadequate to deal with recent changes in labour market supply and demand and which is in the course of revision. As will be seen below, a gradual shift is taking place from a work permit regime to a work visa regime (where the individual is not tied to a particular employer), but in general the more liberal regime is only being applied to high-skills employment where a labour shortage exists.

The shortage of workers with key skills has led to high-profile Government campaigns in 2000 and 2001 to attract suitably qualified foreign workers. A Government-sponsored jobs fair has already visited a number of countries, including Canada, the Czech Republic, India, South Africa and the USA. It will be evident that not all of those targeted are would-be Irish return migrants.

The section which follows describes the principal categories of immigrant workers in terms of the admission regime and related arrangements which apply to them.

Work permits
Definition
Up to the present, Ireland has in general relied on a work permit, not a work visa, scheme. This means that an employer must demonstrate that he/she has a particular need for the worker in question. The logic of the system is that a work permit is therefore granted to a worker to work for that particular employer *and only for that particular employer*. The worker is not free to sell his or her labour on the open labour market. The employer, not the prospective employee, must apply for the permit.

There are a number of exceptions where a work permit is not required by an non-EEA citizen, notably

- persons to whom the new work visa regime applies (see below)
- persons who have been granted refugee status by the Minister for Justice, Equality and Law Reform
- post-graduate students where the work is an integral part of the course of study being undertaken. (This includes post graduate doctors and dentists with temporary registration.)
- non-EEA workers legally employed in one Member State who are temporarily sent on a contract to another Member State ('Van der Elst' case 1994)
- non-EEA nationals married to Irish nationals
- persons with permission to remain as spouse of an Irish national
- persons with permission to remain as the parent of an Irish citizen
- persons who have been given temporary leave to remain in the State on humanitarian grounds, having been in the asylum process
- persons who are posted on an intra-corporate transfer/ secondment for a maximum period of four years to an establishment or undertaking in Ireland that is owned by a company or group that has operations in more than one State
- persons coming to Ireland from an overseas company for a maximum period of three years for training, whether or not it entails remunerated work, at an Irish-based company

The Work Permit Section in the Department of Trade, Enterprise and Employment examines applications from employers and issues permits where appropriate. The fees for a work permit ranges from £25.00 to £125.00 depending on the duration of a permit (maximum twelve months).

Given that it is pertinent for the Irish Government to ensure that employment is available for Irish and other EEA nationals, employers who apply for work permits are generally required to establish that it has not been possible, in spite of reasonable efforts being made, to fill the vacancy with an Irish or other person for whom a work permit is not required. A permit is granted when the employer has no alternative but to employ a non-EEA national.[12]

Social and economic rights of work permit holders.
Work Permit holders have the right to enter employment and reside in the State. Nonetheless, they do not have the right to free medical care and social welfare entitlements. Furthermore, they do not have the right to free education.

Work visas and work authorisations
Definition
To facilitate the recruitment of suitably qualified people from non-EEA countries for designated sectors of the employment market where skill shortages are particularly acute, a *working visa* and *work authorisation*[13] scheme was introduced in 2000. This makes it possible for prospective employees with job offers from employers in Ireland to obtain immigration and employment clearance in advance from Irish Embassies and Consulates. (Immigration Officers retain discretion in specified circumstances to refuse entry to any non-national.)

Applications for *working visas* and *work authorisations* are accepted from persons outside the country only. All of the sectors covered are experiencing substantial labour shortages at present.

• information and computing technologies professionals
• information and computing technologies technicians
• architects, including architectural technicians / technologists

- construction engineers, including engineering technicians
- quantity surveyors
- building surveyors
- town planners
- registered nurses

These visas and authorisations are usually granted for a period of two years by the Irish Embassy or Consulate and can be renewed at the end of that period. While the application must be accompanied by a job offer from an employer in Ireland, holders of working visas and of work authorisations are allowed to change their employers within the same skills category after arrival in Ireland, as long as they continue to have authorisation to work and reside in the country.

Social and economic rights
Work visas or work authorisation allows the person to enter employment and reside in the State. They also have the right to travel if a re-entry visa is obtained before a person leaves Ireland. However, they do not have the right to free medical care and social welfare entitlements. Nor do they have the right to free education.

In general, the holder of a *work authorisation* may be joined by his/her spouse and/or minor dependant children once he/she can show that he/she is in employment. The holder of a working visa must have been in Ireland for three months before he/she can be joined by his/her spouse and/or minor dependant children. The holder of a *working visa* or *work authorisation* must be able to support the family members in question without the need for them to have recourse to public funds or paid employment (unless a family member holds a *working visa, work authorisation* or *work permit* in his/her own right).

Dependant children under the age of 18 are entitled to free primary and secondary education.

Business permits
Definition
Anyone can apply for a business permit. Individuals and companies that are not from a European Agreement country have to invest a minimum sum of £300,000. This condition does not apply to nationals and companies from countries, which have signed Association Agreements with the European Community. They include: the Baltic States, Bulgaria, the Czech Republic, Hungary, Poland, Slovak Republics, Slovenia and Romania.

The association agreements came about following the fall of the Berlin Wall when the European Community took steps to strengthen their relationship with the Central and Eastern Europe countries (CEEC). The intention was to create association agreements 'of third generation' providing a context for aid and assistance to the CEEC and, in the longer term, integration into the Community.[14] The agreements contain articles relating to the exercise of a right of establishment by companies and nationals from each of the Europe Agreement countries. The agreements give them access to and residence on the territory of the Union for self-employed and those seeking to establish themselves as self-employed through a company or as key personnel of a company or firm based in a Europe Agreement country.[15]

Social and economic rights
Individuals with business permits have the right to reside in the State. They only have the right to establish and carry out a business. They do not have the right to medical and social welfare entitlements. Furthermore, they do not have the right to free education.

Rights and protections for foreign workers
Legislation to deal with discrimination in the workplace is still
in its infancy in Ireland, but significant changes have taken
place in recent years. Three principal pieces of legislation are
now in place. Moreover, the Government has also established
powerful new agencies to police the implementation of these
measures. While these changes are broad-ranging in their
implications, there is a primary focus on the workplace.

Prohibition of Incitement to Hatred Act 1989
This legislation is the first of its kind in Ireland. It is directed at
(a) actions likely to stir up hatred (b) broadcasts likely to stir up
hatred (c) preparation and possession of material likely to stir
up hatred. Unfortunately, while well-intentioned, the Act has
proved difficult to apply in practice, largely because the burden
of proof in showing an actual intention to incite hatred is
difficult to establish. In more than a decade since 1989 only a
single case was upheld and it has just been overturned (March
2001) on appeal.[16]

The Minister for Justice, Equality and Law Reform has
already announced (late 2000) a review of the legislation.

Equal Employment Act 1998
The Employment Equality Act 1998, prohibits discrimination
in relation to employment on nine distinct grounds

- gender
- marital status
- family status
- sexual orientation
- religious belief
- age
- disability

- race
- membership of the Traveller community.

With the exception of gender and marital status, complaints of discrimination under any of the other grounds can only be brought in relation to incidents that occurred after 18th October 1999. It will be noted that 'immigrant' is not in itself included in the nine grounds and that the term race (used without inverted commas) is in itself much contested, at least in the English-speaking world. The precise scope of the legislation will in practice be determined by emerging case law.

Where a person considers that s/he has been discriminated against on the gender ground, the Act allows the complainant the option of applying directly to the Circuit Court for redress.

The Employment Equality Act covers employees in both the public and private sectors as well as applicants for employment and training. The scope of the Act is comprehensive and deals with discrimination in work related areas, from vocational training to access to employment and employment conditions generally, including training, work experience and advancement within employment. The publication of discriminatory advertisements and discrimination by employment agencies, vocational training bodies and certain vocational bodies, i.e. trade unions and employer, professional and trade associations are also outlawed.

Equal Status Act 2000
The Equal Status Act, 2000, prohibits discrimination in the provision of goods, services, disposal of property and access to education, on any of the nine grounds referred to under the Employment Equality Act 1998.

The Act outlaws discrimination in all services that are

generally available to the public, whether provided by the State
or the private sector. These include facilities for refreshment,
entertainment, banking, insurance, grants, credit facilities,
transport and travel services. Discrimination in disposing of
premises, provision of accommodation, admission or access to
educational courses or establishments is prohibited subject to
a number of exemptions. The Act also contains sanctions
against private registered clubs that are found to be
discriminating.

Establishment of State agencies to implement new legislation.
Two new agencies, the Office of the Director of Equality
Investigations (www.odei.ie) and the Equality Authority
(www.equality.ie) have been established. While it is still too
early to evaluate the effectiveness of these agencies, what can
be said is that their proactive approach and legislative powers
do give them real power and should enable a new landscape of
equal rights to be mapped out.

*The National Consultative Committee on Racism and
Interculturalism.*
The NCCRI was established in 1998 with the aim of
promoting a more pluralist and intercultural Ireland. It has no
statutory powers and reports to the Minister for Justice,
Equality and Law Reform. The NCCRI is a partnership
organisation that aims to contribute to the overall
development of public policy in relation to racism and to
encourage integral action towards acknowledging,
understanding and celebrating cultural diversity in Ireland.

CONCLUDING REMARKS

Immigration and Integration Policy
Policy to date has been piecemeal and has left it largely to the
market to determine de facto immigration criteria in

individual cases. Changes introduced in 2000 saw a shift from work permits to work visas, but only in the case of a limited number of specific sectors where skill shortages were known to exist. In the meantime, there has been a significant rise in short-term work permits of one year or less, mainly for less skilled labour. The nature of the work permit system, which effectively ties the immigrant to a particular employer, leaves open considerable possibilities for abuse and regrettably there are indications that such abuse is indeed taking place.[17] One has to wonder how the distinction between work visas for the well-educated, high-skilled migrant, and work permits for the less fortunate, can be justified.

Coordination at governmental level is poor as yet. The *Interdepartmental Working Group on the Integration of Refugees in Ireland* produced a groundbreaking report *Integration: a Two-Way Process* in 1999. Taking the theme that 'people from different backgrounds and cultures can enrich the society around them and contribute to the continued development of Ireland', the report was the work of a committee, representing the following Government departments

- Department of Justice, Equality and Law Reform (Chair)
- Department of Education and Science
- Department of Enterprise, Trade and Employment
- Department of Environment and Local Government
- Department of Foreign Affairs
- Department of Health and Children
- Department of Social, Community and Family Affairs.

The report's recommendations include the need for an organisational structure for co-ordinating and implementing policy, the need to raise public awareness, the need to make mainstream services more accessible, and the need to conduct

more basic research. While excellent, the very objectives
chosen by the report provide some indication of how much
ground has yet to be covered. Moreover, consultation with
interested NGOs, community groups and key individuals was
limited and included very few representatives of minority and
immigrant communities. Follow-up has been extremely
limited.

The report, as the title of the working group confirms, was
concerned with refugees rather that the immigrant
community in general. This in turn highlights another
vacuum. While the Department of Justice has perforce been
obliged to address the more urgent issues in connection with
asylum-seekers and refugees, there is a danger that 'normal'
labour market immigrants and their needs are not being
attended to at all. Yet the issues of integration and
multiculturalism raised in the report of the Inter-
Departmental Committee arise in the same way for all
immigrants.

The danger is that a voluntarist campaign, based on elite
discourses and focused on only one segment of the immigrant
population (refugees and asylum-seekers) will fail to achieve
the more fundamental aim of preparing Irish society in general
for the advent of a multicultural society and for the
mainstreaming of multicultural objectives throughout the
range of State policies, programmes and services. All of this
serves to highlight the absence of an inter-departmental
structure with real power, prepared to tackle all of the issues
of immigration, integration and multiculturalism in a
concerted, integrated fashion.

Recommendations/possible areas for future research

• There is a need for better statistical data, more sophisticated
  statistical analysis and more targeted labour market
  projections. These should be published after consultation

with the social partners and academic experts. The exercise should include a national and regional mapping exercise to determine the foreign worker needs of agriculture, industry and the services sector.

- More effective coordination between Government departments is needed. A study of other countries with a view to the identification of best practice models and their modification for Irish conditions is needed

- A comprehensive immigration policy is needed. It should encompass immigrants with a range of skills and should also recognise humanitarian and majority world existing links and needs, while avoiding the encouragement of a 'brain drain' from less wealthy countries. The general replacement of a work permit regime by a work visa regime would be desirable.

- There can be little doubt that a percentage of asylum-seekers could more appropriately be regarded as would-be economic migrants. The institution of some form of quota-based approach for certain countries, possibly introduced in tandem with changes in asylum policy where there is in practice virtually no question of asylum being granted to citizens of particular countries, would be a helpful step forward.

- Family reunification entitlements need to be codified, just, transparent and substantially non-discretionary.

- Elite integrationist discourses currently exist in a vacuum. There is a need to study ways in which these discourses can be related to Irish experience in Ireland and other countries. A balance also needs to be struck between voluntarist and prescriptive approaches.

- Specific pro-immigrant measures should be put in place especially in the fields of information, linguistic support and legal advice.

- Integration policies have relied largely on private-sector, NGO and community initiatives. Consideration needs to be given to this issue. If this approach is to be continued such initiatives should be financially supported by the State through direct funding for NGOs and their operations.
- Mainstreaming integration and anti-racist action is now urgent. It would be over-sanguine to rely on legal instruments and associated caselaw to achieve this, a more proactive approach is now called for. Particular attention should be paid to the role of the educational curriculum.

Notes

1   Government of Ireland *Programme for Economic Expansion* (1958).
2   O'Connell, P. *Astonishing Success: Economic Growth and the Labour Market in Ireland.* ILO Employment and Training Paper No. 44, (Geneva: ILO 1999)
3   Government of Ireland, *National Development Plan 2000–2006* (1999).
4   Department of Finance, *Monthly Economic Bulletin,* March 2001.
5   e.g. the 'marriage bar' whereby women in the civil service were obliged, until 1973, to retire on marriage.
6   Central Statistics Office *Population and Migration Estimates April 2000,* (Dublin: CSO, 2000), p.8.
7   Central Statistics Office (2000) *op.cit.*
8   See 'On target for 200,000 immigrants to take jobs', *Irish Examiner,* 28 March 2001.
9   See, for example, Fanning, B. 'Reluctant Hosts' *Administration* (2001), Keogh, D., *Jews in Twentieth-Century Ireland,* (Cork: Cork University Press, 1998), and the *Reports of the Commission on Emigration and Other Population Problems 1948-1954.*
10 See Keogh, D. (1998) *op.cit*
11 See, for example, Interdepartmental Working Group on the Integration of Refugees in Ireland *Integration: a Two-way Process,* (Dublin: Department of Justice, Equality and Law Reform, 1999)

12   For more detailed information, please see *Changes to Work Permit Requirements in Ireland: Information Note,* available from the Department of Enterprise, Trade and Employment.

13   Work authorisation is granted to persons from any country that do not need an entry visa to enter Ireland. Work visas are granted to persons that do require a visa to enter Ireland.

14   Guild, Elspeth, *A Guide to the Right of Establishment under the Europe Agreements,* Baileys Shaw & Gillett in association with ILPA (1996), p. 2.

15   Ibid.

16   See 'New incitement of hatred act sought', *Irish Times,* 14 March 2001.

17   See, for example, 'Visas for immigrant workers sought by SIPTU', *Irish Times,* 22 March 2001; 'Immigrants treated little better than bonded labour, claims union', *Irish Examiner,* 22 March 2001.

Chart 1 Population of Ireland (26 Counties only), 1841–1981

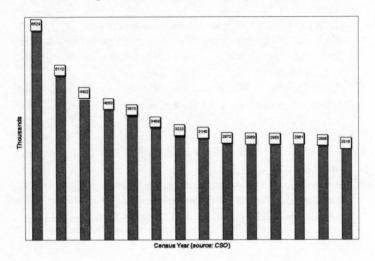

Chart 2 Net migration 1966–1986

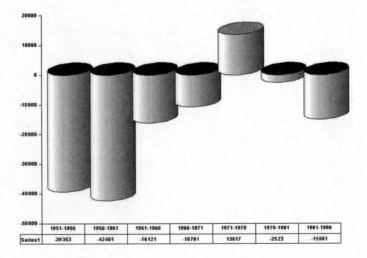

Chart 3 Population increase 1951–1981

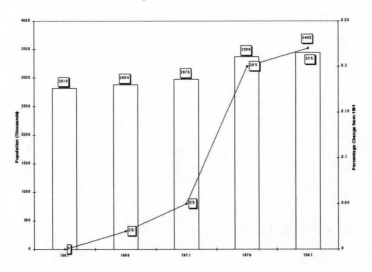

Chart 4 In-Migration and Out-Migration, 1988–1995

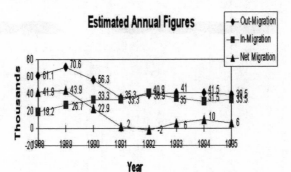

Chart 5 Net Irish Employment Growth, 1988–2000

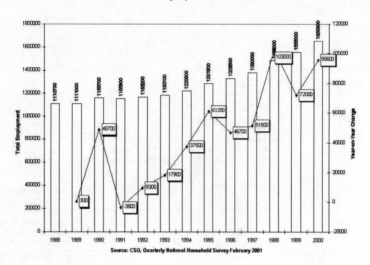

Chart 6 Total Fertility Rate, Ireland, 1960–1980 (source: CSO)

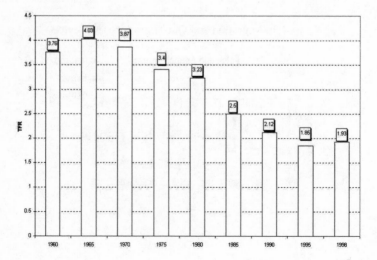

Chart 7 Total Fertility Rates Compared, 1960–1991

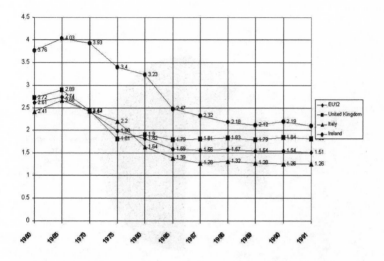

Chart 8 Foreign born residents, 1998 Census of Ireland

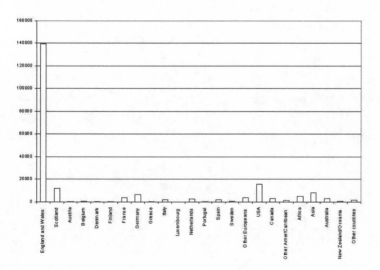

Chart 9 Immigrants to Ireland, 1995–2000 (CSO)

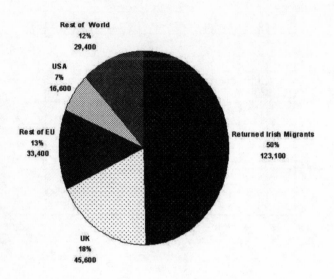

Chart 10 Immigrants by Nationality, 1995–2000

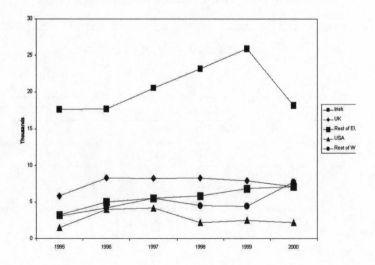

Chart 11 Immigrants by region of origin, 1995–2000

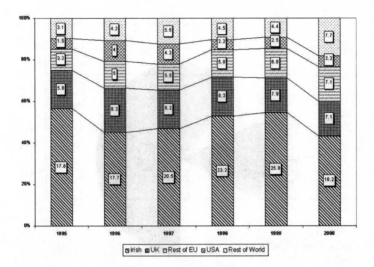

Chart 12 Asylum Applications in Ireland

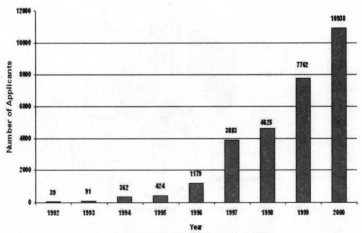

(Source: Department of Justice, Equality and Law Reform)

Chart 13 Work Permits for non-EU nationals

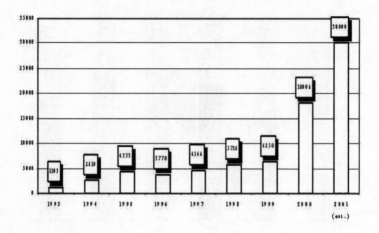

Chart 14 Non-EU nationals working in Ireland, by sector

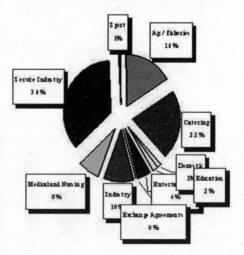

Chart 15 Non-EU Nationals, 2000
(countries with more than 400 nationals in Ireland)

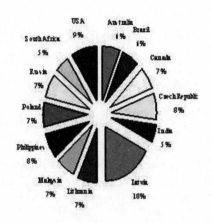

WOMEN AND RACISM

Anastasia Crickley

SOJOURNER TRUTH, a former slave speaking at a rally for women's rights in 1850, caused a lot of discomfort by proclaiming:

> And ain't I a woman? I have ploughed and planted and gathered into barns . . . Nobody ever helped me into carriages, or over mud-puddles, or give me any best place. I have borne thirteen children and the lash as well . . . Ain't I a woman?

Her words are still relevant a century and a half later. In speaking of her experiences, she articulated differences based on gender, ethnic and class oppressions, as well as their combined reinforcing of one another. In today's Ireland and today's world the intersection between gender and class oppressions and racism poses a major challenge for all concerned to acknowledge, promote, protect and respect women's rights as human rights.

The need to protect and promote women's rights as human rights is now widely recognised in various global, European and national policy and legislative agendas, although practice and implementation procedures still lag behind at all levels. The UN

Convention on the Elimination of All Forms of Discrimination against Women (1979), which Ireland has ratified, also makes a clear statement about racism,

> the eradication of apartheid, all forms of racism, racial discrimination . . . is essential to the full enjoyment of the rights of men and women.

Furthermore the Platform for Action – agreed by the 189 member states of the United Nations at the Third Global Conference on Women in Beijing (1995) and reinforced in the review process (2000) – both copper-fastens women's rights as human rights and makes a clear commitment to:

> intensify efforts to ensure equal enjoyment of human rights . . . for all women and girls who face multiple barriers to their empowerment through race, age, ethnicity, culture.

These commitments are reinforced by EU Directives and Irish anti-discrimination legislation (the Employment Equality Act 1989 and the Equal Status Act 2000), yet the day to day realities of the interaction between racism and gender oppression spoken of by Sojourner Truth continue to mar the lives of women from minority ethnic groups in Ireland and elsewhere.

In the rest of this short article I will outline some brief snapshots of how this intersection between racism and gender oppression can be experienced, discuss some of the issues raised by these experiences for feminists, anti-racist groups and all committed to contributing to a fair, just and equal society, and finally draw some conclusions regarding possible strategies and actions.

In attempting these tasks, I will be drawing on my involvement and work with Traveller women through Pavee

Point and the National Traveller Women's Forum, and with black Irish women and women from other minority ethnic groups through the National Consultative Committee on Racism and Interculturalism. I will also draw on my own experience some time ago as a woman migrant in Britain and the deliberations of many women globally who have explored these issues.

I also acknowledge my position as a non-Traveller and, in Ireland, a white member of the dominant ethnic group, but with thanks to the many women who have helped shape my external understanding of their reality. We all have a responsibility, I believe, to help create the conditions to transform and transcend oppression and to examine our own – sometimes unconscious – roles in its maintenance.

Experiences of racism and gender dimensions
The implications of this crosscutting oppression experienced as a woman, as a member of a minority and as a woman member of a minority – this triple burden so to speak – have been spelt out clearly for us by woman from a variety of backgrounds both in Ireland and elsewhere. Their stories are complex also, demonstrating clearly that just as women are not a homogenous group neither are the women of a minority ethnic groups homogenous, and their stories are not new.

Margaret Maughan writing of her experience as a Traveller woman in 1989 said:

> Settled women look down on Traveller women and give out about them for the oppression that they suffer. But what a lot of settled women don't see is that Travelling and settled women are in the same boat when it comes to the way they are looked down on and treated in society by men.

In the work with Traveller women we have found that the immediate reality of racism and discrimination for Traveller women – often perpetuated by 'other' settled women as Margaret points out – and for Travellers as a whole group, inevitably means that this external oppression takes priority.

In effect, the pervasiveness of external oppressions make these the major priorities for all group members including Traveller women. It also becomes very difficult to prioritise the gender dimension of this oppression. For example, adequate and appropriate accommodation is required urgently by all Travellers. But Traveller women, because of their homemaking roles, are most acutely affected by the lack of accommodation, sanitary and water facilities. However, the forms of accommodation campaigns and government resources are more likely to be accommodation issues overall.

Equally I am conscious that many of the issues affecting working class and marginalised women, while they do have a gender dimension and one that needs to be addressed, are issues that affect social welfare provision and general class oppression. Finally, Traveller women blamed, as Margaret Maughan puts it, for their own oppression, blamed in effect for being Travellers, feel constrained to defend somehow their right and the right of all travellers to exist as Travellers.

The external oppression and racism from the settled population, which is the daily experience of all Travellers including Traveller women, inevitably takes precedence over internal oppressions. However, this is not to say that internal oppressions are ignored, as the Pavee Point Domestic Violence Programme can indicate. But responses to feminist issues are often ambivalent.

The complexities and contradictions Traveller women experience in dealing with the intersections between gender and ethnic oppression are mirrored in the lives of women from other minority ethnic groups. As Beverly Bryan and her colleagues put it:

> We do have to deal with things like rape and domestic violence, and black men are as sexist as the next man… but if you are a black women, you've got to begin with racism, its not a choice, it's a necessity.

As Ireland moves from being a land of outward emigrants to a host society for immigrant workers, refugees and asylum-seekers, many of our new arrivals are women. The structural and institutionalised nature of the intersection between racism and gender oppression, present across the spectrum, is particularly evident in the global experiences of migrant, refugee and asylum-seeking women.

Having entered a country as the partner of a migrant worker, or applied for refugee status recognition as part of a family group, their individual rights may be at best invisible or at worst entirely dependant on their male partners' status. The services they receive and the application processes they go through may, consciously or unconsciously, show no particular sensitivity to their gender background or lives as women, in effect leading to experiences of racism for them. Regrettably, women from the new communities say that these forms of racism, however unintentional, are part of their daily lives in Ireland.

Discussion
Women's experiences of racism are constituted differently, as the above examples indicate, depending on their own different class positions and different positions within global relations of power. While there is no doubt that the diplomat's wife could experience racism, and that there may be some similarities in

aspects of her experience with that of the asylum-seeker woman, there are also major differences in the experiences and how, in general, they affect the life chances of both women.

Secondly, again as the above examples indicate, women have long since striven to articulate their particular experiences and priorities in addressing racism and gender oppression and to formulate feminist ideas in line with these. These ideas challenge and continue to challenge all concerned, as feminists are, with the liberation of women.

Feminism

I describe feminism as theory and practice that acknowledges the oppression of women and seeks to transform this situation. There are various ideas about this process, various strands of feminist theory – liberal, radical, socialist, black, spiritual – and various approaches to feminist practice, which reflect similar division. Feminist theory and practice have not, either, been free of ethnic and class bias. Agendas set around equality of access to education, training, jobs and pay are seen to have benefited mostly white, settled, middle-class women. The poverty and marginalisation of working-class women, though given verbal space, have not achieved the same focus, or anything like the same results.

Initially, women from subordinate ethnic groups found themselves rendered invisible within the women's movement, and racism towards them continued in the struggle for universal liberation for the 'universal women'. Patricia Hill Collins in her book *Black Feminist Thought*[1] states the position clearly:

> Theories advanced as being universally applicable to women as a group, on closer examination appear greatly limited by the white, middle-class origins of their

proponents and … promote the notion of a generic
women who is white and middle class.

She might have added that such theories also promote notions
of women as sedentary and Western in orientation. She does
go on to give a long list of such theories, including the classical
works of Nancy Chodrow and Carol Gilligan on mothering
and the moral development of women respectively.

Further discussion of the inter-relationships between
white/dominant ethnic groups superiority and white
superiority is continued below, focusing on internal and
external oppression.

External oppression

Addressing internal oppressions, in the face of what may be
experienced as all out class or cultural attack is, as all the
experiences listed indicate, extremely difficult. However, as I
have already suggested regarding Travellers' accommodation,
external oppressions have a gender dimension and they cannot
be adequately addressed if that gender dimension is ignored.
The feminisation of poverty and the way it differentially affects
women and single parent families, mostly headed by women,
has been well documented.

What could be called the feminisation of racism means that
Traveller, black, refugee, asylum-seeker and other minority
ethnic group women suffer oppressions experienced by the
whole group more acutely. The appalling living conditions
experienced by Travellers mean that nearly all Traveller women
suffer miscarriages, still births or lose small children. Black Irish
women are invited to go back home and subjected to sexualised
racist remarks and attacks at the same time. Women from the
new communities are treated the same as the men from their
communities without sufficient account being taken of their
specific and additional needs

In all cases in my experience, a clear analysis of the gender dimension of poverty and racism is required. Questions, such as why do women suffer this way, and how can we ensure that anti-poverty and anti-exclusion programmes do not further marginalise women (as indeed was the case with some early aid programmes) need to be posed and responded to. In effect, analyses and actions against poverty and racism need to specifically name and include women, otherwise they do actually aid their oppression

Internal oppression

The reality of the gender dimension of external oppression for women from subordinate ethnic groups does not, however, remove internal gender oppression and the need to address it. Margaret Maughan and Beverly Bryan are clear that Traveller and black men can be sexist too. In ethnic groups under attack from external dominant groups, oppressive control of female sexuality may be seen as a way of maintaining group boundaries as well as providing males in the group, already themselves oppressed everywhere else, with ways of exercising some domination.

Heidi Hartmann, defining patriarchy, maintains that it involves a set of hierarchical social relations between men that allow for the control of women. Even men at the bottom of the pile have direct control over some women, which, it could be argued, helps keep the male hierarchy in place. Women in subordinate ethnic groups may be forbidden contact with (especially) men from other groups, or even outside their own direct families; have little or no choice with regard to marriage arrangements; and have all of their movements curtailed by a male-controlled hierarchy. Sexuality may be also defined in rigidly heterosexist terms leading one to assume for example that there are no Traveller lesbian/gay people whereas it may

be the case that these have been forced to pretend not to exist
even more than in the dominant sedentary group.

Internal oppressions objectifying women

Women from different cultures and different classes may
differently prioritise the gender oppressions from which they
need liberation. In particular, white, settled middle-class
women – being relatively free of external class and racist
oppressions – can more readily focus on issues of individual
choice, freedom and sexuality. However, all women know the
experience of internal gender oppressions. Women from
subordinate ethnic groups need support to name the
oppressions they know, and define their own priorities and own
strategies around addressing them.

Gender oppressions are destructive of women, limiting their
potential and casting them in roles as each others keepers – it is
frequently the older women in subordinate ethnic groups who
enforce group rules regarding the control of female sexuality,
thus finding their own power and making the process of
liberation more difficult. A 'process of liberation' that allows
for the continuation of women's oppression is impossible, in
my view, to define as fully liberating.

Thus, an end to racism cannot be achieved without also
challenging abuses of women's human rights that reinforce
male superiority in the name of cultural forms. This challenge
can only succeed when it is from and with, rather than for,
women from minority ethnic groups themselves. But that is
not to say gender oppression is the same as racism or that one
should ignore human rights abuses for fear of interfering with
'culture'.

Racism

Racism, the combination of prejudiced belief in the inferiority
of other ethnic groups, the power to act out of that belief and

through it to justify bad treatment, discrimination and hatred, is well discussed elsewhere in this book. The reality that racism can be conscious or unconscious, institutional or individual is also dealt with and has been touched on here. Historically, through processes of slavery, colonisation and marginalisation, there have been clear links between racism and sexism and the particularities of women's experience of the intersection between the two, which they throw up – some of which Sojourner Truth articulated earlier. But the struggle to make visible women's racism, not as an add-on but as a key issue to be addressed, remains ongoing.

Conclusion

The issues discussed above are not new, but they are particularly pertinent if Ireland, which is increasingly multi-cultural, is to move from being a stagnant, unwilling host society for migrants and others towards an intercultural society. Creating an intercultural society is the responsibility of all, but the greatest responsibility must rest with the most powerful individuals and institutions – through our laws and leaders as well as through our daily practices, procedures and jokes and the images portrayed for us through our media.

To create a society free from racism necessitates that the racism experienced by women is named and addressed. Again, this is a challenge for all, but there is a particular responsibility for the most powerful at all levels as is discussed above. The rights of minorities within minorities cannot be ignored even when they challenge the power of majorities within the minority as well as the power and dominance of the majority ethnic groups overall.

Not ignoring the racism experienced by women means naming it and addressing it not just in articles and publications on women and racism but in every article, action, discussion and strategy against racism. All actions against racism need to be gender proofed with women's racism mainstreamed directly with their consideration. And all current attempts at gender mainstreaming need to include a particular focus on women from minority ethnic groups. Otherwise actions against both racism and gender mainstreaming are in danger of contributing to, rather than alleviating, the oppression experienced by women from minority ethnic groups. Not an easy starting point, brothers and sisters, but an essential one.

Notes

1. *Black Feminist Thought*, Patricia Hill Collins, Unwin and Hyman, London (1990)

HEALTH AND RACISM:
A TRAVELLER PERSPECTIVE

Ronnie Fay

Equity has been defined as a fundamental principle of Irish health policy. Increased funding, commensurate with the scale of the issue, should be allocated to tackling the unacceptable health status of the Traveller community and the widespread obstacles to Traveller access to health services

Task Force on the Travelling Community, 1995

Introduction

IRISH TRAVELLERS are a small indigenous minority group (approximately 0.5 per cent of the national population) who have been part of Irish society for centuries. They have a value system and language, customs and traditions that make them an identifiable group. Their distinctive lifestyle and culture, based on a nomadic tradition, set them apart from the sedentary population.

Travellers' separateness, partly by choice, enables them to retain their identity as an ethnic group in the face of much opposition and pressure to conform to sedentary society. Their experience of low social status and exclusion – which prevents them from participating as equals in society – is mostly due to the widespread hostility of settled people towards them. This hostility is based on prejudice, which in turn gives rise to discrimination and affects Travellers in all aspects of their lives.

Health profile

> From birth to old age those at the bottom of the scale have much poorer health and quality of life than those at the top. Gender, area of residence and ethnic origin also have a deep impact.
>
> *The Black Report, UK 1980.*

In 1983, the Travelling People Review Body proposed the regular and systematic collection of data on the health status of Irish Travellers. The publication of the 'Travellers' Health Status Study – Census of Travelling People 1986' (Barry and Daly, 1988) and 'The Travellers' Health Status Study – Vital Statistics of the Travelling People 1987', (Barry et al, 1989) gave rise to considerable concern about the health status of the Traveller community. These reports found that:

- fertility rate of Travellers in 1987 was 34.9 per thousand – more than double the national average and the highest in the European Union
- Travellers have more than double the national rate of still-births
- infant mortality rates are three times higher than the national rate
- Traveller men live on average ten years less than settled men
- Travellers are only now reaching the life expectancy that settled people reached in the 1940s
- Travellers of all ages have very high mortality rates compared to the settled Irish population

- Traveller women live on average twelve years less than their settled peers
- Travellers have higher rates of morbidity for all causes, and their death ratio is significantly higher than the general population for:
  Accidents
  Metabolic disorders in the 0–14 age group
  Respiratory ailments
  Congenital problems

Issues impacting on the health status of Travellers
The issues around health are inextricably linked to issues regarding appropriate accommodation provision for Travellers, and to the social and economic exclusion of this community within contemporary Irish society. The context of Travellers' lives includes the stress generated by living in a hostile society where discrimination is a constant reality; this is compounded by frequently enforced change in their way of life. These factors impact adversely on Traveller health and negatively affect their experience of the health service and their ability to influence and access same.

Pavee Point
Pavee Point – formerly Dublin Traveller Education and Development Group (DTEDG) – was established in 1983 and is a non-governmental organisation committed to human rights for Irish Travellers. The group comprises Travellers and members of the majority population, working together in partnership to address the needs of Travellers as a minority group who experience exclusion and marginalisation. The overall strategic aim of Pavee Point is to contribute to an improvement in the quality of life of Irish Travellers.

The work of Pavee Point is based on an acknowledgement of the distinct ethnic culture of Travellers, and the importance of nomadism to the Traveller way of life. Innovation has been a key feature of the work done from its starting point based on a community development approach, an inter-cultural model and a Traveller/settled partnership. It means working with, rather than for, Travellers in a manner that prioritises Traveller participation. The organisation seeks to combine local action with national resourcing, and direct work with research and policy formulation.

Pavee Point Traveller Health Initiative
Since its establishment, Pavee Point has worked to identify and highlight the multi-dimensional nature of the marginalisation and social exclusion of Travellers, and has sought appropriate ways of facilitating improvements in the situation. While the issue of health was always one of major concern within the organisation, it was not until the early 1990s that the possibility of engaging in targeted actions to promote improvement in Traveller health arose. In 1991, Pavee Point received FÁS funding to deliver a 'New Opportunities' course to a group of Traveller women, some of whom requested more focused training in health care at the completion of the course. A proposal was submitted by Pavee Point, in consultation with these women, to the Eastern Health Board for the setting up of a Primary Health Care Project for Travellers. This project aimed to co-ordinate and manage, in partnership with the Eastern Health Board, a Traveller Health Promotion service for Travellers. The proposal was accepted and the Primary Health Care for Travellers project was set up in October 1994. Although Pavee Point has engaged in separate health development work for Travellers since that time, the Primary Health Care project has been the main channel through which related actions have taken place.

The Primary Health Care (PHC) for Travellers Project

The PHC project has the following objectives:

- to establish a model of Traveller participation in the promotion of health
- to develop the skills of Traveller women in providing community based health services
- to liaise and assist in creating dialogue between Travellers and health service providers
- to highlight gaps in health service delivery to Travellers and work towards reducing inequalities that exist in established services

Primary Health Care

Primary Health Care has been identified and used as an innovative approach to health care in the developing world. In the last decade there has been a growing interest in and demand for such a service in the developed world, as evidence from studies indicate that the expanding marginalised populations here are suffering disproportionately from poor health and have less access to health care services.

Primary Health Care is a statement of health philosophy, it is not a package, or a complete, defined methodology. It is a flexible system that can be adapted to the health problems, the culture, the way of life and the stage of development reached by the community. Successful primary health care projects have emphasised a process that valued empowerment, partnership and advocacy when designing and implementing health care interventions. This allows the partners to highlight inequity and negotiate solutions with their relevant partners. Community participation and partnership are key requisites for the success of Primary Health Care.

Community participation

The approach inherent in the project is to work 'with' the Traveller community in order to develop a Primary Health Care project – based on the Traveller community's own values and perceptions – that will have long-term positive outcomes.

In the context of the Primary Health Care for Travellers project, community participation is viewed as a process through which Travellers will gain greater control over the social, political, economic and environmental factors that determine their health. The Traveller community must participate in every stage of the project from the initial assessment of the situation; defining the main health problems/issues; setting priorities for the project; implementing the activities and monitoring and evaluating the results.

Partnership

For Primary Health Care to be effective, there must be close collaboration between the Traveller organisation, the health sector and a range of other statutory and voluntary agencies. The value of this partnership between Pavee Point and the Eastern Health Board is that it has demonstrated that it is an effective model and is impacting positively on the health condition of Travellers in the pilot working area. The different strengths and resources of the statutory and voluntary sectors, brought together in a constructive way on an agreed agenda, have more impact than if either operated in isolation. Each partner brings different skills to the project. Pavee Point provides the channel of communication and established trust with Travellers, an arena for Traveller participation and a community development approach to working with Travellers. The Health Board provides the funding, the health knowledge and the health professionals.

A crucial ingredient for this partnership has been a willingness to dialogue, as equals, while respecting each others roles, responsibilities and ethos.

The Primary Health Care Project

> For achievement worthy of international recognition, this WHO 50th anniversary commemorative certificate for a national community-based health project that promotes health for all, values of equity, solidarity, participation, intersectoral approaches and partnership is awarded to the 'Primary Health Care for Travellers Project, Dublin, Ireland.
>
> *JO E. Asvall, M.D. Regional Director, WHO Regional Office for Europe, September 1998*

The project included a training course that concentrated on skills development, capacity building and the empowerment of Travellers. This confidence and skill allowed the community health workers (CHWs) to go out and conduct a baseline survey to identify and articulate Travellers' health needs. This was the first time that Travellers were involved in this process, in the past their needs were assumed. The results of the survey were fed back to the community, they prioritised their needs and suggested changes to the health services that would facilitate their access and utilisation. The results were also fed back to the health service providers; a joint workshop took place between the Traveller community and the health providers where an agreed set of priorities and interventions were drawn up. The health workers then set about implementing these interventions. This was a very effective process as it facilitated the participation of the community in defining needs, setting priorities and outlining interventions and it provided baseline data on the current access and use of services. The community and the CHWs felt that it empowered them. They now feel that they have control over what is happening to them, as they are involved in an ongoing process that they can feed into. This process has been critical to the success of the project as people are engaging and are confident to articulate their needs. One of the findings of the survey was the lack of appropriate health information on what services existed and how, where and why you could access them. This lack has been addressed through the project, and has led to an increased uptake of the health services.

Interventions and outcomes of the project to date

• Greater awareness has been created about the needs, entitlements and possibilities in the health services, as well as the difficulties accessing services that should be available.
• Sixteen Traveller women have received accredited training as Community Health workers and are currently employed on the project, funded by the Eastern Health Board.
• Training, planning and implementing interventions in:
  Public health nursing
  Oral health
  Nutrition
  Environmental health
• Culturally appropriate health education materials have been designed by the project. To date, posters have been produced covering topics such as Travellers' health status; breast feeding; care of burns; immunisation; nutrition and oral health. These posters deliver key health messages in a culturally appropriate way; they increase Traveller visibility in education materials and can be displayed in surgeries and clinics.
• Research on Traveller women's reproductive health and the production of a training video and accompanying information booklet.

- Organising well-woman clinics specifically targeted at Traveller women. These clinics have facilitated access for the first time for Traveller women to cancer screening and family planning facilities. These special clinics will be supported on an interim basis, while the Traveller women build up confidence and knowledge of the service. During this period the project will also be lobbying for the provision of this level of service in the local area.
- Networking with Traveller organisations, at national and local levels, to pass on information and resources on the health issues facing Travellers and outline the process and outcomes of the project.
- Providing in-service training to a range of health professionals that aims to encourage health personnel to offer a more culturally appropriate service and work towards an increase in the utilisation of essential services.
- The process of facilitating community participation in the project has resulted in the empowerment of Travellers and led to them taking more control of their health situation. Their attitudes to the health system have changed through the provision of information, training and resources, which in turn has brought about a change in their ability to access the system. They are making greater demands on health services and have greater expectations for the health services to be provided in culturally appropriate ways.
- Organising health education sessions on-site, delivered by the CHWs, has made health information more accessible and culturally appropriate and addresses the language and culture gaps that exist.
- Advocacy and lobbying are core actions of the PHC project. In order to lobby for the policy changes needed to promote the recognition of the special needs of Travellers and their inclusion in all mainstream provision, a number of

submissions to relevant Government policy papers and
reports were prepared by the project.
- Representation and participation by the project on a range
  of national and regional advisory committees and working
  groups, including the Eastern Health Board Traveller Unit,
  the National Health Network and the National Traveller
  Health Advisory Committee. The task of this committee is
  to draft a National Traveller Health Policy to reflect the
  analysis in the report of the Task Force on the Travelling
  Community.
- Organising regular seminars and conferences with health
  service providers to highlight the situation of Travellers
  health and to create space to discuss challenges and
  mechanisms to address these issues with a view to
  increasing equality of outcome for Travellers in relation to
  their health status.

Through Pavee Point's experience of working on health – both
from the direct work on the project and from our involvement
at national level over the last six years – challenges that need to
be addressed if we are to ensure equality of access,
participation and outcome by Travellers in the health service
have emerged.

THE CHALLENGES

- **The provision of culturally appropriate health care for
  travellers**
  Health Services need to be flexible in their delivery in order
  to respond to the needs of Travellers, but the criticism is
  often made that the provision of culturally appropriate
  services is expensive and requires additional resources. In
  the main, it may just be about using your resources in a
  different way to increase the impact of the service.

Additional resources may be necessary in the short term to set up the service, but once established they are more effective and reduce cost in the long term.

- **Participation of Travellers and Traveller organisations in health policy, planning and services**
  The current planning structure treats everybody equally. This responds to the needs of a certain proportion of the population, but it presumes that the population is equal and has equal levels of literacy, language, education, information and physical and financial services. Therefore, it excludes special needs groups. Health Services need to be challenged to be flexible in the delivery of services to these groups. This can be done by facilitating the participation of Travellers and Traveller organisations in the planning process and the delivery of services.

- **The provision of targeted and mainstream health responses**
  'Targeting' or affirmative action is required to counter past disadvantages in addressing the health needs of Travellers. It can enable Travellers to develop their analysis and understanding of health issues, and thus develop more control over their own health agenda. Targeting creates the conditions for mainstreaming, which is an essential part of the solution for Travellers' health status. Mainstreaming does not mean integration into existing services, it means that services change so that they are relevant and accessible to both Travellers and other minority ethnic groups, as well as to the majority population. It means we have ethnic pluralism in health where health provision is intercultural.

- **Changing the status of Travellers in Irish society**
  Changing the health status of Travellers requires not just a health care strategy. A much broader ranging strategy is

essential. Issues of citizenship and participation; education and employment; poor accommodation and inadequate services; racism, sexism and other forms of discrimination have all to be addressed. Health strategies need to impact on these issues and be coordinated and integrated with them. It requires coordination, information sharing, dialogue and co-operation between a variety of actors and sectors. Multidimensional strategies are required to address the health status of Travellers in a manner that address and removes root cause. In addition we need to recognise and respond to the diversity of needs within the Traveller community.

- **To acknowledge the need for the identification, collection and collation of desegregated data for Travellers in the health services**
  Currently, due to the lack of desegregated data it is very difficult to plan provision of health services effectively or to measure equality of access, participation or outcome for Travellers' health. In the Task Force Report it was pointed out that the planning process of services was being seriously hampered by this lack of accurate data. The report recommended the putting into place of mechanisms to identify, collate, and analyse data on the access and outcomes for Travellers of the various services including health, education and training, taking cognisance of the data protection implications.

  Since the Task Force Report was published Pavee Point has developed initiatives in this area. Our Integra project, in partnership with the Department of Education and Science and FÁS piloted the development of administrative procedures, including ethnic monitoring and tracking mechanisms. Our health programme has been working on the piloting of an ethnic question to identify Travellers on the RICHS (Child Health Record System) with the Eastern Health Board.

Pavee Point believes that these systems have the potential to contribute significantly to the improvement of outcomes for Travellers in the health services. However, it has to be done within a framework of overall ethnic monitoring as part of a strategy to mainstream equality in service provision.

Recommendation to respond to the challenges

- *Ethnic Equality Monitoring.* The Department of Health and Children should devise a system of identifying Travellers on all health record systems within the context of ethnic equality monitoring. These figures, alongside information from census data, can be used to assist in planning services and identifying gaps in provision of health services to Travellers.
- *Supporting Targeted Initiatives.* These should include: Traveller health advocates or community health workers; mobile clinics; specialist public health nurses, etc. Traveller health advisors providing resources, in appropriate ways.
- *Mainstreaming Travellers and Traveller issues into all policies and services.* This will involve introducing a Traveller proofing mechanism into all dimensions of the health service. Policy development and the implementation of services should be assessed on their ability to include Travellers and respond appropriately to their needs. Travellers must be named in all documents relating to health policy. The explicit naming of Travellers as a specific group with specific needs and concerns will go some way to ensuring that they are included in all strategic plans. This recommendation is based on the principle that where Travellers are not named, their distinct needs remain unmet.

- *Initiatives to address the specific needs of particular groups of Travellers.* This should include a focus on women, older Travellers, youth, and Travellers with a disability
- *Facilitating the employment of Travellers in health services.* This should include the use of identified positions as recommended by the Task Force, with special access criteria applied to certain jobs serving the Traveller community to increase the chances of Travellers taking these posts, e.g. child-care workers; refuge staff; as community health workers. Affirmative action programmes are also required in creating training channels where it would be possible for Travellers to be employed as nurses and doctors, for example. These would include having reserved places on courses; special bursaries; and awards for training institutions.
- *Effective participation of Travellers and Traveller organisations in policy development and the prioritisation and application of resources.* This would involve partnership in the activities of health institutions. It would mean adequately resourcing Travellers and Traveller organisations to participate meaningfully at all levels, i.e. needs assessment and prioritisation; planning and design; implementation and evaluation. It means creating additional positions for Traveller organisations on regional and national committees, so support can be provided for Traveller representatives to engage effectively in the process, while acknowledging the imbalance in the power relationships. It is only in this way that a truly responsive health service will be achieved, that is a service that is based upon and led by health service user needs.
- *Health advocacy needs to be identified as a role for health institutions.* As demonstrated earlier, the living conditions and economic circumstances of Travellers particularly affect their health status. A key priority and principle of any

Traveller health strategy must be to recognise the role of health institutions as health advocates. This would require a commitment to ensure that the Department of the Environment, and the local authorities, have a role in developing health/safety standards for the design of Traveller sites.

* *In-service training should be resourced and prioritised.* All health professionals as part of their vocational training should have an introduction to Traveller culture and issues. The focus for this training should ensure the development of the skills necessary to provide an inter-cultural service and ensure an anti-racist context.

    – Specific ongoing training modules should be developed and supported for health personnel working with Travellers.

    – Local Traveller groups – supporting/resourcing/informing their involvement in developing partnerships and encouraging their participation.

Conclusion

There are currently very positive indicators and opportunities for change that the statutory and Traveller organisations have to exploit. There is the changing context in relation to the new equality legislation and the establishment of the equality authority. In the area of Travellers' health there is a growing commitment at all levels to address the health status of Travellers, with the establishment of the National Traveller Health Advisory committee and the Traveller Health Units at regional level. Since 1998, additional resources specifically targeted for Travellers health have been realised from the Department of Health and Children, and a National Policy on Travellers health is being prepared by the national committee. New understandings, new commitments and new approaches have taken time to develop. Efforts and commitment can only be maintained if concrete change for Travellers materialises in a very short time. However, the task is to ensure these mechanisms are working effectively to create change and not to underestimate the needs, the urgency and the challenges.

Intercultural Education
and the School Ethos

Donal O'Loingsigh

WHILE IT IS TRUE to say that the Republic of Ireland joined the European Union almost thirty years ago, it has remained for most of that time an essentially mono-cultural society, one that is based primarily on the values and culture of one dominant group. For this reason, Ireland has traditionally made little or no provision for the culture of other groups, including minority ethnic groups.

However, society is forever changing and evolving and the increasing secularisation of Irish society is no exception. In addition, the changes brought about in recent years by the ever increasing numbers of non-EU ethnic minority communities arriving in Ireland, principally as refugees, asylum-seekers and economic migrants means that substantial adjustment in the structure of Irish society is inevitable.

This adjustment has implications for every sector of Irish society, but especially for education. The lack of provision for any culture other than that which is perceived as the culture of the dominant group is obvious in our society. But it is the lack of provision for cultural diversity in our education system, especially at primary level, and in our actual school structures that I want to focus on in this chapter.

In particular, I want to highlight the number of structural barriers that inhibit active or real participation by ethnic minorities in the education system.

Let us look for a moment at what happens and what is allowed for under the present structures. Traditionally, provision for education in Ireland has very much followed strict denominational lines. In reality, this meant that if you were Roman Catholic you went to the local Roman Catholic school, if you were Protestant you went to the nearest Protestant school. Under the present structures, the primary system in the Republic of Ireland only allows for two types of school: denominational or multi-denominational.

State funding for non-denominational schools is actually prohibited by our constitution. Except for a mere eighteen multi-denominational schools scattered throughout the larger urban areas and the one Jewish and one Muslim school in Dublin, the vast majority of the other 3200 primary schools are Roman Catholic schools, leaving only a tiny minority of Protestant schools.

It is both unlikely and impractical to expect that all the various ethnic minorities arriving in Ireland in recent years would establish schools that would meet their own religious and cultural needs. Therefore, the reality is that they are going to be educated mainly in the existing denominational schools, which as I have pointed out, are mainly Catholic. At the same time, Ireland has both a moral obligation and a legal duty to cater for the needs of all within those schools. This has tremendous implications for these schools in terms of change in management structures, in terms of change in ethos and in terms of the resourcing of these schools.

If, as a nation, we are to meet our obligations both morally and as an EU member and adhere to EU and UN policy and legislation that relates to the recognition and provision of multi-cultural education and equality of access to education for children of ethnic minority communities, then, not only will the very structures on which our education system is founded have to change, but also the culture and ethos of many of our schools. I will refer more specifically later in this chapter to culture and ethos and their importance in creating a totally inclusive society

One of the ways that people's rights can be recognised and protected is by having them enshrined in legislation. The passing of the Education Act (1998), the Employment Equality Act (1999) and the Equal Status Act (2000) should, in theory, secure the rights of all. But will they? I do not believe that such legislation will necessarily be sufficient to meet either ethnic or minority needs, because the enactment of legislation in itself cannot legislate for moral obligations. Legislation must be accompanied by significant attitudinal changes if minority rights are to be adequately protected.

There are also practical difficulties in implementing legislation effectively. Take, for instance, the Education Act, which relates specifically to schools and educational institutions. How can the rights guaranteed under legislation be enforced when the structures and resources are not in place to do this effectively? For example, how is the issue of parental choice to be addressed? The Education Act (Section 6e) states that the right of parents to send their children to a school of their choice should be promoted. What real choice is offered to parents of ethnic and religious minority children under our present structures?

The reality is that the present education system in Ireland has a limited range of choices mainly based on denominational grounds. A further question is the information available to parents of children of ethnic minorities on which choices can be made. When we speak of parental choice, it should be an informed choice, one based on correct and adequate amounts of information. How can parents of minority ethnic children make this informed choice when there is a dearth of information and advice available to them and no adequate structure in place to provide them with it?

Despite the fact that Article 42.1 of Bunreacht na hÉireann acknowledges the family as the primary and natural educator of the child and despite the ever growing body of evidence that recognises the importance of parental involvement in a child's education, there are no structures being put in place to involve the parents of ethnic minority children in the existing education structures or to educate parents of these children about our system.

The Education Act (Section 6k) also states that the language and cultural needs of students, having regard to the choices of their parents, should be catered for. One of the primary vehicles through which culture is transmitted and preserved is language. While accepting that everyone has a need to understand, speak, read and write the dominant language used in society, every child should also have the right to maintain his/her cultural and linguistic identity. Underlining this is the right of every child to learn his/her mother tongue. How, under the present structures, can schools realistically hope to implement these objectives? In order to reconcile these two objectives an all-embracing intercultural education policy in relation to diversity and the teaching of language is needed. Without a significant increase in resources in terms of language teaching resources, availability of specialist language teachers and in terms of the professional development of teachers in the area of intercultural education, it will not happen.

The Education Act (Section 6b) further states that there should be made available to all people resident in the State a level and quality of education appropriate to meeting the needs and abilities of those people. Currently, it is extremely difficult for children from ethnic minorities to learn to value their culture, their traditions, their language and way of life when the schools they attend are traditionally dominated by one culture and no effort is made to prevent the minority cultures from being subsumed / assimilated into the mainstream culture. While this situation is the result of a lack of understanding of the needs of ethnic minorities rather than a deliberate school policy, it still is the reality for nearly all our religious and ethnic minorities in our education system at the moment. To change this position an intercultural approach to education is needed.

Intercultural education is an education for both the minorities and the majority community in Irish society. It is about realising that in society there is a culture and set of values that belong to the majority, but other minority groups have a different culture and set of values; while they are not the same as the values of the majority they are equally important and valid. Intercultural education must aim to ensure the integration of ethnic minority children, while at the same time ensuring that these children do not lose their ethnic identity and cultural values.

For the majority it is mainly a matter of learning to live in a multicultural society, to respect and accommodate diversities and to realise that everyone has the right to maintain his/her cultural and linguistic identity. It is not about integrating ethnic minorities into our culture so that they become 'more Irish than the Irish themselves', but rather about educating people about tolerance, human rights, democracy and, most of all, respect for difference. This process should start in the early years and permeate throughout the entire education system.

Returning to the culture and ethos of schools and their importance in creating a totally inclusive society, one of the essential conditions for the development of respect and tolerance for diversity is the creation of an affirming school ethos. While ethos is a very nebulous term and one which is difficult to define, if we define ethos as the dominant, pervading spirit or character of a place constitution, then in relation to intercultural education we are talking about an ethos that genuinely values each child, including their cultural and religious heritage. Schools that strive to create such an environment, in which the positive worth of each individual within the school, both children and teachers, is valued and recognised are more likely to achieve the type of ethos necessary to tackle successfully the questions of racism and culture.

The creation of such an environment must be the priority of all schools and the role of the principal in the development of and affirming this type of ethos is crucial. However, can such an ethos be compatible with the ethos of a denominational school, the type of school the vast majority of our ethnic minorities are obliged, by circumstances to attend? And if not, what are the consequences for the ethnic and religious minorities? Catholic schools, for example, are obliged under the 'Deed of Variation' to:

- manage the school in accordance with the doctrines, practices and traditions of the Roman Catholic Church
- make and keep themselves familiar with the ethos of the Roman Catholic Church and the Roman Catholic Faith, insofar as the same relates to education and schools
- manage and cause the School to be managed in a manner which will uphold and foster such ethos
- not do anything or permit anything to be done in relation to the School, or the management thereof, which would have or would be likely to have a detrimental effect on the Roman Catholic Ethos of the School

It is therefore evident that the question of interculturalism needs to be accommodated, and that the rights of ethnic and religious minorities must be realistically and adequately catered for in the current Deeds of Variation for Denominational Schools.

Furthermore, Section 37 (i) of the Employment Equality Act confirms this view for me:

> A religious, educational or medical institution which is under the direction or control of a body established for religious purposes or whose objectives include the provision of services in an environment which promotes certain religious values shall not be taken to discriminate against a person for the purposes of this Act, if:
>
> a It gives more favourable treatment, on the religion ground to an employee or a prospective employee over that person where it is reasonable to do so in order to maintain the religious ethos of the institution, or
> b It takes action which is reasonably necessary to prevent an employee or a prospective employee from undermining the religious ethos of the institution.

The reality then is that the patrons of denominational schools – including the Jewish, Muslim, Presbyterian and Church of Ireland schools, as well as Roman Catholic schools – are legally entitled to take whatever action necessary to prevent the undermining of the religious ethos of their respective schools.

Therefore, while the numbers of religious and ethnic minorities attending denominational schools are in the minority and do not threaten that school ethos their presence will be tolerated, but once their numbers increase significantly as they inevitably will, particularly if they are concentrated in certain areas, I believe attitudes to their presence could quickly change.

Providing an intercultural education that incorporates equal recognition to other religions appears to be incompatible with the ethos of a denominational schools. Thus, I believe that the creation of a truly intercultural educational system in Ireland demands far reaching structural changes in how schools are both established and managed. There should be no need for new schools. The 3,200 or so primary schools in the system at present are more than adequate to accommodate our falling school population. What we need is that Churches, through the patrons of our existing denominational schools, would agree, where necessary, to a shared management structure for schools that enrol pupils from ethnic and religious minorities. This would mean sharing the management, on an equal basis, with other denominations. Surely with sufficient goodwill the already existing post-primary concept of a community school could be extended to primary level.

I am not in any way suggesting whole scale reorganisation of schooling along these lines, nor am I suggesting any interference with the rights of parents who wish their children to be educated in a denominational school of their choice, but I believe there are opportunities in the whole of Ireland – North and South – for the Churches to consider the value of mixed schooling. Equal involvement of all in joint management would be in the overall interests of communities that are becoming more multi-denominational and multicultural by the day.

Without this change – which would mean major concessions for all involved – the present system will lead to one or other of the following, given the reality that non-denominational state funded schools are not allowed under our constitution: we will either have, at enormous and unnecessary cost to the state, a huge increase in the number and diversity of minority denominational schools or, preferably in my view, a massive increase in the number of new schools through the multi-denominational sector.

Finally, let us hope that these changes in our educational system will take place sooner rather than later, so that the values of inclusiveness, accountability and respect for diversity expressed in the Education Act will be recognised and implemented in our schools and classrooms. But for this hope to be realised a significant shift in the structure, culture and ethos of our educational system will have to take place before we can have meaningful intercultural education in our schools.

References

Fullan, M., *The Meaning of Educational Change*, New York: Teachers' College Press, 1982.

Government of Ireland (1938), *Bunreacht na hEireann*, Dublin: Stationery Office.

Government of Ireland (1998), *The Education Act*, Dublin: Stationery Office.

Government of Ireland (1999), *The Employment Equality Act*, Dublin: Stationery Office.

Government of Ireland (2000), *The Equal Status Act*, Dublin: Stationery Office.

PART THREE

RESPONDING TO RACISM

THE MEDIA AND RACISM

Nuala Haughey

JOURNALISTS HAVE RESPONSIBILITIES when it comes to covering issues involving ethnic minorities, and the duty of a free press in a democracy is an ethical one. Indeed the very first rule in the National Union of Journalists' (NUJ) Code of Conduct, which its members are bound by, is that 'a journalist has the duty to maintain the highest professional and ethical standards'.[1]

Many of the stories that Irish journalists cover are driven by a desire to unearth wrongdoing, duplicity and double standards in public life or to highlight injustices. These are among the more noble of journalists' endeavours.

When it comes to racism, the ethical issue is clear. Our union stands full square against it. Journalists have a duty to not be racist, just as we have a duty to not be sexist or ageist, in our reporting. The NUJ's Code of Conduct tells us to think carefully about the words we use and only to mention a person's age, race, colour, creed, disability, marital status, gender or sexual orientation if this information is 'strictly relevant'. It states that 'a journalist shall neither originate nor process material which encourages discrimination, ridicule, prejudice or hatred on any of the above-mentioned grounds.'[2]

The guidelines on reporting race relations actually go even further than this by encouraging members to actively seek through their work to expose the myths and lies of racist organisations and their anti-social behaviour. We also have specific guidelines on the coverage of stories involving Travellers, which say journalists should strive to ensure that nothing they write could lead people to the view that Travellers are less than full citizens of the State.

Guidelines and codes of conduct are essential, but they are pretty useless if they are not implemented. Unfortunately, sections of the Irish media have been consistently flouting best practice in their coverage of the asylum/refugee issue in the past few years. While I use the word media to encompass all its forms, my focus in this paper is on the print media as this is the area I am most familiar with.

We have seen, and are still seeing, ill-informed, unbalanced and sometimes inaccurate reporting as well as sensationalist and careless headlines. But we are also seeing well-informed, balanced, accurate reporting with measured and careful headlines.

The failure of some sections of the media to live up to the standards set by their union and expected of them by society are well documented by now, so I won't dwell too long on examples. But here are a few of the more alarming, and alarmist, recent headlines:

'Refugee tried to bite me to death'. This was the front page lead story of *The Sunday World* in February 2000. This exclusive report was about a young Irish mum whose refugee husband from Kosovo attacked her like 'a wild animal'. This headline, and the accompanying story, attempted to dehumanise the refugee husband, in much the same way as other tabloid headlines dehumanise sex offenders by turning them all into beasts.[3]

The Irish regional press too has been found wanting on the issue. On 29th July 1998, *The Wexford People*, after the arrival of forty-seven Romanians in a freight container in the port of

Rosslare, carried a front-page editorial claiming the 'latest influx' of asylum-seekers had brought public services in the town to 'breaking point'. The editorial also peddled the usual urban myths about worries that young male asylum-seekers would deliberately impregnate local girls to get residency status here and that the new arrivals were dressed in designer clothes.[4]

An *Irish Times* colleague, Andy Pollak, carried out an interesting study that concentrated largely on coverage of the asylum/refugee/'race' issue in 1997 by the Independent Newspapers Group, which dominates the print media market.[5] The Independent Group's titles include the largest circulation national daily newspaper, the *Irish Independent*, the only Dublin evening paper, the *Evening Herald* as well as the *Sunday Independent* and the *Sunday World*. The group also has a major share holding in the only homegrown tabloid, the *Star*, as well as a minority share in the *Sunday Tribune*.

Pollak examined the output from some of these papers during 1997, an election year when the refugee story began to take off as the numbers of people claiming asylum in Ireland started to grow significantly.

He noted how, from the outset, the *Irish Independent's* emphasis was on an alleged link between bogus refugees, criminals, welfare fraud, prostitution and begging. Most of the stories on this subject were and still are written by the paper's security correspondent and most rely on Department of Justice or Garda sources.

In May 1997, a year when the total number of asylum applications topped only 3,883, the *Irish Independent* was reporting 'growing fears' by immigration officials that 'the country is on the brink of a major refugee problem.'

Other headlines in 1997 documented by Pollak include:

'Floodgates open as new army of poor swamp the country', from the *Sunday World* in May.

'Crackdown on 2,000 "sponger" refugees', in the *Irish Independent* also in May.

'Refugee Rapists on the Rampage', the *Star*, on 13th June, in a story in which 'top Garda sources' warned Dublin women to stay away from refugees after a spree of sex assaults by rapacious Romanians and Somalians.

The same story appeared in the *Irish Independent* on the same date. Both reports were based on the comments of an unnamed police officer in Fitzgibbon Street Station in Dublin.

'Dublin now main target for gangs trafficking in people' and 'Shopkeepers say theft by Romanians is snowballing'. Both these headlines come from the *Irish Times* in May 1997. Such reports have undoubtedly negatively influenced public discourse on the refugee issue and encouraged a 'them and us' attitude to the State's newest ethnic minorities.

In his study, Pollak pointed out that the real problem in the asylum area in 1997 was administrative paralysis in government, not excessive numbers. This paralysis had been noted by a Trinity College Dublin academic, Rosemary Byrne, in a book on discrimination and refugee law.

Byrne's theory was that the government failed to deal efficiently and fairly with applicants for refugee status in a reasonable time frame. She noted that it had allowed those with no valid claim for refugee status to remain in the State, thereby fuelling misinformed intolerance towards the broader community of asylum-seekers and refugees.

The State's administrative problems in autumn 1999 led to scenes of asylum-seekers queuing chaotically for hours outside the Refugee Applications Centre in Dublin. These scenes, combined with a lack of clear political leadership on the issue, certainly contributed to a climate of resentment and served to leech public sympathy from asylum-seekers.

The screaming headlines we can all point to and deplore. But also worrying are the less sensationalist stories which nevertheless bolster the authorities' presentation of the increase in the asylum-seeker population as a security problem.

The stories which newspapers like the *Star* and the *Irish Independent* regularly carry about 'bogus' asylum-seekers 'flooding' the State are based on information from powerful sources, usually from the Department of Justice or the Garda Síochana. While journalists using irresponsible language must be held accountable, the usually unnamed officials who feed sensationalist stories to their favourite hacks should also be challenged. Politicians and journalists know the importance of language, yet both can be careless about how they use it.

Take, for example, the inaccurate use of the term 'illegal immigrants' as a generic category that includes asylum-seekers. Asylum-seekers are not illegal immigrants; they enjoy the protection of the State while it is deciding on their claim for refugee status. But calling them 'illegals' is a way of suggesting they are not deserving of our resources, our support, our sympathy.

Then there's the statement that four out of five asylum-seekers are not genuine. This statistic has been repeated mantra-like by government politicians and their spokespeople. Yet we don't hear the same politicians drumming up statistics like, for example: four out of five self-employed people are tax cheats, four out of five social welfare claimants are dole fraudsters, four out of five banks overcharge their customers or four out of five inmates in Irish prisons come from socially deprived areas. We wouldn't hear such phenomenon boiled down to sound-bites because it does not suit the governing parties to trumpet such calculations on those sorts of issues.

It does suit them, however, to cast the asylum-seeker in
the role of the undeserving outsider in our midst. The
language politicians use to set the narrow boundaries of the
asylum debate is passed on, through the media, to the
public.

Small wonder, then, that when Department of Justice
Equality and Law Reform officials visited towns and villages
last year in advance of the dispersal of asylum-seekers, they
were faced with fierce resistance from some host communities
based, in part, on the hostile propaganda that officialdom had
had a hand in creating.

But back to journalism. There are positive examples among
many media organs of stories that attempt to grasp, and deal
fairly with, the complexities of the asylum/refugee situation
and to highlight racism. The *Sunday World,* which produced the
'Refugee tried to bite me to death' headline in 2000, had an
altogether different image of a refugee in an inside article in
April 2001. It read: 'Bullied teen is aiming to be Ireland's first
black Olympic champ.' The story focused on a sports enthusiast
African girl in Tallaght, County Dublin, who is regularly subject
to racist abuse.

In the wider immigration field, the media rightly took the
authorities to task over the poor treatment of nineteen
Moldovan workers who were led to court in handcuffs after
being detained at Dublin airport in possession of valid visas and
work permits in January 2000. The jobs the men had come to
take up had fallen through. They were released by the courts
after several days and were offered alternative employment, but
their plight highlighted shortcomings in the system of dealing
with immigrant workers. Following their release the Minister
for Justice, Equality and Law Reform, Mr John O'Donoghue,
swiftly announced new arrangements to allow for temporary
admissions in similar circumstances. In this case, journalists

asked the uncomfortable questions and printed photographs of the men being led to court handcuffed to prison guards.

So how can we improve the overall situation, remembering as we must that journalists do not work in sociology departments, that they have strict deadlines and often have to make snap decisions on angles or tones of stories?

There are various possibilities and I'll outline them briefly:

Complaint handling

Complaint handling is an area where there would certainly be scope to address readers' concerns on an ongoing basis, so that ethical discussions could become part and parcel of a media outlet's daily dialogue with its consumers.

The newspapers that are members of the National Newspapers of Ireland (NNI), including the main dailies and Sundays, already have in-house readers' representatives. These are supposed to provide quick and easy access for readers to voice their complaints and obtain remedies such as corrections, retractions or apologies. They work, it has to be said, with varying degrees of success.

Such an internal system for dealing with readers' complaints clearly cannot provide the same degree of public accountability as an external independent adjudicator.

An external complaints-handling system could address complaints about press standards that have been made to the newspaper itself, but which cannot be resolved by it. This could take the form of the appointment of either a press ombudsman or a press complaints commission to enforce an agreed code of practice.

The NUJ favours a non-statutory media ombudsman funded by media owners and answerable to a media council drawn from the social partners. This person would deal with complaints as well as having an educational role.

The NNI favours the establishment of an independent system of press complaints, or self-regulation, also funded by the industry. The commission would be made up of a commissioner who would decide in a particular case whether the code had been upheld or breached, would try to resolve complaints, and could make recommendations and require the newspaper to publish his or her determination on whether there has been a breach of the code.

Self-regulation, instead of a form of regulation imposed by the government, is obviously likely to get more support from the industry. It would also recognise the fact that responsibility for newspaper ethics lies with journalists and publishers rather than the government.

So if the journalists' union and the newspaper industry's body are in favour of an external complaints handling mechanism, why isn't it happening? Basically, the answer is that the industry wants libel reform, and says the setting up of a press complaints body is contingent on changes to our archaic libel laws. Since 1991, when libel law reform was first recommended by the Law Reform Commission, nothing has changed. We are still awaiting the heads of a bill on libel reform, which the Taoiseach said would be ready in winter 1999.

There are other steps that could be taken that don't require legislation. They include:

Education
Journalists, like everyone else, need to be educated on 'race' issues. We need our employers to invest in training us. We need to ask questions, have open minds and be prepared to have our opinions challenged. We can do this informally or formally and at local and national level.

We also need to employ journalists from a variety of ethnic backgrounds in our newsrooms. RTÉ recently appointed interns from minority ethnic groups and such people undoubtedly bring a new perspective on issues.

Ideas that could be discussed include the National Newspapers of Ireland joining together with the NUJ for a joint initiative on racism. The National Consultative Committee on Racism and Interculturalism could play an important role in lending its expertise for some sort of training initiative.

Empowerment of minority ethnic groups
Often reports on the asylum/refugee area lack input by the people affected by the stories because the journalist does not have any contacts in the refugee or ethnic community who can supply a sound bite on the topic of the day.

Because of the reliance by many journalists on powerful sources for information and stories, there is no real pressure on them to change this situation. But if help was offered to minority groups to develop a media profile and appoint articulate spokespeople, they could make an impact in the news agenda. Members of refugee and ethnic minority lobby groups should be funded to allow them to equip themselves to join in public debates through the media, to challenge policy, set agendas and to allow their experiences to be heard. Travellers' organisations have shown how effective such strategies can be.

Conclusion
The NUJ's Irish organiser, Seamus Dooley, has pointed in the past to a factor that is outside the control of our individual members. That is, the impact of the market on the decisions of media managements on how they treat news and features. Dooley has said the NUJ is gravely concerned at the influence of market forces on the quality of news and current affairs coverage and the seemingly unrestrainable drive to satisfy the lowest common denominator in terms of populist

sensationalism. He said at a conference: 'The NUJ is firmly opposed to the treatment of news and current affairs as just another marketable product which can be bent and shaped to fit the demands of the consumer society. Indeed if there is a responsibility on individual journalists to educate themselves on the handling of race-related stories, there is an even greater responsibility on media owners to resist the temptations of market share to sensationalise.'

The responsibility to cover developments in the refugee/asylum/'race' area ethically and fairly extends from media owners to individual journalists, politicians and policy-makers, officials, trade unionists, NGOs, the Churches and the public, including minority ethnic groups. We each have a role and an obligation to fulfil it.

Footnotes
1.   National Union of Journalists' Code of Conduct
2.   National Union of Journalists' Code of Conduct
3.   *Sunday World*, February 6 2000
4.   *The Wexford People*, 29 July 1998
5.   Pollak, Andy, *An Invitation to Racism? Irish Daily Newspaper Coverage of the Refugee Issue in Media in Ireland: The Search for Ethical Journalism*, Dublin: Open Air, 1999

RACISM, POVERTY AND COMMUNITY DEVELOPMENT

Hugh Frazer

I have the audacity to believe that people everywhere can have three meals a day for their bodies, education and culture for their minds and dignity, equality and freedom for their spirits

Martin Luther King

THERE IS A COMPLEX and multi-faceted connection between racism and poverty. Not all poverty involves racism and not all racism involves poverty. However, there can be no doubt that racism can cause and exacerbate poverty and that poverty can cause and exacerbate racism; the one cannot be tackled without tackling the other. Martin Luther King recognised this in his campaigns for civil rights and racial justice in the United States. Thus he also struggled against poverty and economic and social exclusion. We need to do the same in Ireland.

Addressing the connection between racism and poverty cannot happen in isolation from changes in the wider society. If the specific actions identified in this chapter are to be effective, they need to be part of a wider effort to combat racism throughout Irish society. This wider context involves working to change attitudes and structures in society and ensuring and rigorously enforcing a strong legislative basis for tackling discrimination, promoting equality and upholding basic rights. This wider context is addressed by other contributors to this book. Therefore this chapter concentrates on the links between poverty and racism and argues for two things that would help to break this link. These are:

- fostering a community development approach; and
- mainstreaming an anti-racism dimension in Ireland's (and Europe's) National Anti-Poverty Strategy and related government policies and programmes.

Poverty and racism

When looking at the link between racism and poverty, one of the most striking things in the Irish context is the lack of hard information or data on the position of ethnic minorities, with the possible exception of the Traveller community. However, there is little reason to assume that the experience of Travellers or the pattern that is apparent in Northern Ireland, Great Britain, many EU Member States and the United States of America for other ethnic minorities is not occurring here. Racism is almost certainly an increasing cause of poverty.

To understand the link between poverty and racism we need first to understand what we mean by poverty. The National Anti-Poverty Strategy defines poverty as:

> People are living in poverty, if their income and resources (material, cultural and social) are so inadequate as to preclude them from having a standard of living which is

regarded as acceptable by Irish society generally. As a result of inadequate income and resources people may be excluded and marginalised from participating in activities which are considered the norm for other people in society.

There are three important dimensions to this definition of poverty. These are:

- poverty is understood as being relative – it is related to the living standards prevalent in the society in question. This implies that poverty involves a degree of inequality that excludes some people from what is considered to be a normal standard of living in that society. Thus poverty is seen as being primarily the result of structural faults in society and not the result of the failings of particular individuals or groups. This understanding focuses attention on the main systems that mediate the distribution of resources and opportunities in society, namely the labour market, the education system, the tax and social welfare system and the provision of public services and the extent to which they are fair and treat everyone equally;
- poverty is recognised as being multi-dimensional – it means that people's social, emotional and cultural needs as well as their material or physical needs are being inadequately met. Thus to tackle poverty requires addressing all these aspects;
- poverty involves exclusion and marginalisation. This means that people are marginalised from production (employment), consumption (income), social networks (family, neighbours and community), and decision making. It limits people's ability to participate fully in society. This raises issues of powerlessness, lack of choice, alienation and dependency. It implies that people living in poverty are not

able to access their full economic, social and cultural as well as political and civil rights. It can thus involve partial or limited citizenship.

Racism is an abuse of power. It means treating people as inferior or less capable on the grounds of their race, colour or ethnic difference. It results in discrimination against people and the denial of their fundamental rights. Racism thus can cause and exacerbate all three of these dimensions of poverty. It can curtail people's access to resources and opportunities. It can damage people socially, emotional and culturally as well as materially. It can exclude and marginalise people from full participation in society. These connections between racism and poverty are elaborated on below.

Racism, whether emanating from an individual, a group or an institution, can directly limit people's access to or benefit from the main systems of resource distribution in society. These have been identified in the government's National Anti-Poverty Strategy (NAPS) as fourfold: the labour market, the education system, the tax/social welfare system and the provision of public services.

Access to the labour market
First, in terms of the labour market it is clear that ethnic minority groups often have more difficulty accessing the labour market and experience higher levels of unemployment and indeed, in the case of the most recently arrived asylum-seekers, are not permitted to access it. Where they are successful they are disproportionately likely to be in low-paid, insecure and unskilled jobs in areas such as catering, health services, hotels and repairs. In general they are more likely to be involved in part-time work and shift work, to work longer hours and to have less access to training. There are a number of reasons for

this. Recruitment practices can wittingly or unwittingly be biased against people from ethnic minority backgrounds. Immigration policy can often be focussed on recruiting people from abroad to fill low-status jobs that can't be filled internally; this is particularly likely to occur in a booming economy. However, it is also important to note that some ethnic groups have been specifically targeted to fill skilled vacancies, such as people from the Philippines and India into nursing and IT respectively. This is a positive development, but as the economy slows there may be a danger of racist accusations that they are taking 'our jobs'. Experience from other countries suggests that it is very hard for the children of immigrants to move on to better jobs. They are found disproportionately often in the same jobs as their parents. The extent to which class structures and a lack of social mobility are compounded by racism is thus significant. Racist assumptions about the inferiority, lack of skills or capacity of ethnic minorities can result in refugees and asylum-seekers finding it difficult to access areas of skilled work that their qualifications and experience suggest they should be in. In other cases there may be prejudice against the traditional skills of minority groups. Yet others such as certain groups of asylum-seekers can of course be denied the right to work thus condemning them to dependency and an inadequate income.

Access to education
A key factor in being able to access well-paid jobs is access to good quality education and training. Institutional racism takes place where there is insufficient provision made for the particular educational and training needs of ethnic minority groups and an assumption that the system established to meet the needs of the dominant white majority is sufficient. For newly arrived groups, language barriers and a lack of information on rights, entitlements and opportunities in the

relevant language are often critical factors in accessing employment but also in terms of accessing other services such as the emergency services and participating generally in society. Without specific state educational initiatives to overcome this barrier, ethnic minorities will be significantly disadvantaged. Many refugees and migrants have often experienced disrupted education and again, unless this is specifically recognised and special provision made, they will be severely disadvantaged in many different respects. Furthermore, even if children have access to the normal state education system, there is a wide body of research that shows that parental involvement is a critical factor in how they achieve. Thus support to parents of these children is essential if they are not to be disadvantaged compared to children from a majority background.

There are many other ways that racism can contribute to educational disadvantage. A child's way of life or home traditions may not be validated in school. Because of language difficulties and racist attitudes, assumptions can be made about the ability of children and they can be labelled as 'problem children'. Logistical difficulties such as transport problems can affect attendance, for example Travellers' sites being located far from school. The home environment (e.g. lack of space and facilities for home-study, or parents having to work at night in take-aways and having no one to take care of the child, so the child has to go to the work place and is thus tired at school) can mitigate against educational participation and the state may not address these issues. Teachers may not have access to anti-racist or cultural awareness training, or the necessary supports to teach ethnic minority children.

Tax/social welfare system
In terms of the social welfare/taxation system, racism can occur if people from ethnic minorities are treated differently or

less well than other people. If they have to sign on in a particular place because of their ethnic origin or status, or if they receive different payments (e.g. direct provision and a low payment denying choice as is the case for some asylum-seekers), or if information about entitlements is not in a language that they can understand or is not available to them where they are, then they will be at greater risk of being on an inadequate income and condemned to live in poverty.

Access to public services

In terms of housing and accommodation, ethnic minorities can often be discriminated against, particularly in a very competitive housing market. Racist attitudes denying access to appropriate accommodation, including opposition to Traveller accommodation and accommodation provision for refugees and asylum-seekers, all exacerbate the problem. This can lead to overcrowding or concentration in poor-quality housing and accommodation often in unpopular, hostile, remote or inconvenient areas where it is cheaper in relative terms. As numbers increase, and as a result of the fear of racist attacks, there can be a tendency to concentrate in particular areas. From this the ghettoisation and marginalisation of ethnic minorities can increase with all the consequences of isolation and multiple deprivation. The system of direct provision for asylum-seekers takes away their ability to make choices, fosters a sense of difference and alienation and impedes involvement with local communities.

Problems of access to other services such as health services can be further compounded by racism. If services do not address issues such as the barriers caused by language or lack of information, do not set out to identify and cater for the particular health needs of minority groups through a process of ongoing consultation and research, do not consider culturally specific provision and do not train staff on working with minority ethnic communities, then health inequalities will be compounded. The poor health status of Travellers – very high infant mortality and low life expectancy – is well documented.

As well as limiting people's access to the main system of resource distribution, racism often results in a rejection and denial of the culture and traditions of ethnic minorities. Both at an individual and state level there can be a lack of attention given to ensuring access to appropriate cultural, social and recreational activities and facilities. Cultural policy can unduly reflect a mono-cultural society and fail to give due value to other traditions and cultures and the promotion of an intercultural society. This can interact with economic deprivation and further isolate and alienate and increase exclusion and marginalisation from society. The past history of Northern Ireland alone should be enough to warn us of the dangers of such a narrow racist approach.

The process of exclusion can be further compounded by the marginalisation of ethnic minorities from the political system. This can be reflected in both the failure of political parties to involve and adapt themselves to ethnic minorities and lack of opportunities for ethnic minorities to be part of the many fora where planning and decision-making takes place in society. If all those systems do not consciously take on an anti-racist agenda then they will inevitably exclude. This further limits participation in society and adds to exclusion and poverty.

The connection between racism and poverty can of course be two-way. Clearly, racist attitudes are not peculiar to any one section of the population and are found throughout our society. This is evident from local campaigns against accommodation for refugees and asylum-seekers or halting sites for Travellers as well as more academic research. However, the victims of economic and social inequality who are excluded and alienated from mainstream society are often particularly vulnerable to being exploited by people with racist prejudices. The long-term unemployed person, the young unemployed person, the isolated and neglected older person, the unskilled with few opportunities, those living in inadequate housing or in a poor physical environment, those living in communities experiencing multiple disadvantage – i.e. those with little hope, little chance of progression and a deep sense of insecurity and threatened identity, and those who feel that the booming economy is passing them by – can be especially susceptible to racist propaganda. This spurious propaganda can blame ethnic minorities for the poverty of others (e.g. 'they have taken "our" jobs, "our" housing, "our" welfare') and represent them as a particular threat that may further weaken people's precarious command over resources and opportunities in society. Two things follow from this. First, combating poverty and social exclusion in the wider society must be an integral part of breaking the link between poverty and racism. Secondly, building solidarity between ethnic minorities and other disadvantaged and excluded groups is an essential task. This is particularly where promoting community development approaches comes to the fore.

Why community development?
Community development is a 'process whereby those who are marginalised and excluded are enabled to gain in self-confidence, to join with others and to participate in actions to change their situation and to tackle the problems that face their community'.[2] It involves working collectively for social change that will improve the quality of their lives, of the communities they live in and of the society of which they are part. It is a process that challenges injustice and discrimination and promotes equality, social solidarity and social progress. It thus

involves working for change at three levels: the personal level, the community level and at the level of public policy.

Community development involves a wide range of different types of activity, including personal development and community education projects that foster creativity and self-confidence, women's groups, cultural and community arts projects promoting self-expression and a positive sense of identity, information, advice and advocacy work, campaigning for better services and facilities, tackling local problems like drugs or crime, developing community based services and facilities, developing the social economy, attracting additional resources and investment into an area, improving communication within and between communities.

The importance of community development projects for individuals and groups experiencing poverty and racism is clear-cut. Community development is a way of challenging racism and discrimination and promoting social solidarity. For instance, community development is about:

- addressing the powerlessness and isolation of individuals and ethnic groups experiencing racism. Community development is about building from the ground up. It is about recognising, respecting and developing an analysis of people's experience – in this case the experience of racism and discrimination. Countering racism involves building the self-confidence of those who are its victims and, over time, through collective action building a sense of power and the ability to challenge and change things. It is an alternative to a 'charity' model of doing things for people without understanding their different cultural traditions;
- ensuring that the collective voice of minorities is heard. Tackling racism requires the voice of ethnic minorities to be heard and their experience and needs to be articulated by

themselves. This can only happen through a community development process that builds the social capital of ethnic groups so that they develop the organisations and networks that allow them to influence and change the decisions that affect their day to day lives;

- influencing and changing public policy. The creation of strong representative organisations built from the ground up is essential if the needs of ethnic minorities are to be heard in the policy-making process. They are essential to enable participation and involvement in the various fora where policies and programmes are developed. Such participation can provide opportunities to challenge and change racist attitudes, processes and structures. It will mean that agencies can be challenged to adjust their programmes and procedures to meet the needs of ethnic minorities rather than ethnic minorities being expected to change to meet institutional practice;

- building social solidarity and a respect for difference and diversity in society. A key part of community development is about building solidarity and self-confidence within and between communities (of interest as well as geographic). This in turn builds the self-confidence and strength to look outwards and to start to build alliances and networks with other groups on a basis of mutual respect and equality, for instance between Travellers and other ethnic minorities. This can then lead on to increased awareness of and respect for difference and diversity;

- ensuring that all groups in a community are involved in and part of the development of that community. By emphasising inclusiveness a community development approach can ensure that ethnic minorities are involved in strategies to rejuvenate and improve the quality of life of the areas in which they live and can ensure the development of specific

initiatives aimed directly at the inclusion and integration of
ethnic minorities including refugees and asylum-seekers.
• promoting a respect for the rights of minorities.
  Community development is about confronting
  discrimination, inequality and injustice and ensuring that
  people are able to access their human rights (economic,
  social and cultural as well as civil and political);
• challenging racist attitudes amongst the settled white
  majority. Racism is a problem of and for the white
  majority. There is a need for all community development
  projects to face up to this and to consciously challenge
  misinformation and racist attitudes as a core part of their
  work. Community development projects can challenge the
  fear of difference or a 'foreign culture' through creating
  opportunities for interaction, through highlighting
  commonalities and through developing a shared analysis
  and understanding of racism and of the causes of poverty
  and social exclusion.

Of course, none of this is new. Over the last decade there
have been many projects involving Travellers that have adopted
a community development approach. Indeed it is noticeable in
the work of organisations like Pavee Point, the Irish Traveller
Movement and various local Traveller projects supported under
the Department of Social, Community and Family Affairs'
Community Development Programme, the Local Urban and
Rural Development Programme and the EU Peace and
Reconciliation Programme, that a community development
approach has been dominant. This is in contrast to earlier
approaches, which often adopted a 'charity' model. These
earlier projects tended not to acknowledge and understand the
distinctive Traveller culture and not to involve Travellers
directly in policy and planning. As a result they often adopted

inappropriate responses, for example in areas such as accommodation and education.

Mainstreaming anti-racism

This is a critical moment for anti-poverty policy in Ireland and for ensuring that the link between racism and poverty is clearly addressed in mainstream policies to tackle poverty. All EU Member States are required to submit a National Action Plan against poverty and social exclusion (NAPincl) to the EU Commission. Parallel to this, a major review of Ireland's National Anti-Poverty Strategy (NAPS) is currently underway to review targets and actions under the existing priority themes of unemployment, income adequacy, educational disadvantage, rural poverty and urban disadvantage. In addition, new core themes of housing/accommodation and health and three cross-cutting themes – older people, women and children – have been added. Existing anti-poverty targets and actions under each of these themes are to be revised and new targets are to be considered for the additional themes. In addition there is a specific commitment in the Programme for Prosperity and Fairness (PPF) that 'the NAPS analysis will be updated to include emerging causes of poverty (e.g. racism)'.

There are four overarching things that will be necessary if an anti-racism dimension is to be effectively mainstreamed in policies to combat poverty. These are:

• making anti-racism a strategic objective of each government department and agency and putting in place anti-racism training for all staff;
• collecting data on ethnic minority groups and monitoring their take up of services provided by government departments and agencies;
• building an anti-racism dimension into the guidelines for poverty-proofing that are currently being reviewed by the National Economic and Social Council;

- consulting and involving groups representing minority ethnic groups in the development, delivery and review of services so that there is an appropriate balance between ensuring equal access to mainstream services, where necessary providing 'bridging' or outreach services to enable better access to the mainstream and, where different or special needs exist, providing specialist services.

More particularly the needs of ethnic minority groups should be treated as a cross-cutting theme in the implementation of all the strands of the National Anti-Poverty Strategy (NAPS) (i.e. education, unemployment, adequate income, health, housing/accommodation, rural poverty, urban disadvantage). This will identify specific factors affecting minority ethnic groups as well as consider the causes and effects of poverty generally under these themes. Where appropriate, additional or specific policies and programmes that are necessary to address these issues for ethnic minorities should be identified and clear targets and indicators set for measuring progress on eliminating poverty for these groups.

There is not the space here to elaborate on all the issues and policies in relation to racism and poverty that need to be addressed as part of the National Anti-Poverty Strategy. However, the following are just an indication of some of the issues that will be important:

- ensuring that all people are treated equally by the social welfare system for however long they are in the country. In other words, moving from a system of direct provision and allowances for some asylum-seekers to providing a basic welfare payment for all;
- allowing all refugees and asylum-seekers the right to work after six months while their cases are being considered so that they are not living in poverty;

- ensuring that, where necessary, minority ethnic groups have access to English-language training, access to information in their own language and, when appropriate, translation services;
- facilitating increased access to information, advice and legal services;
- ensuring that mainstream educational provision takes into account different cultural traditions, addressing issues of racism and racial bullying in schools in a proactive manner and providing more educational opportunities within ethnic minority communities, especially opportunities for adults to re-enter education;
- ensuring that health and social services are provided in ways that make them accessible and relevant to the needs and cultures of ethnic minorities, such as recognising the need for gender sensitivity whereby women are seen by female medical staff, ensuring access to GPs, facilitating eligibility for medical cards and publishing and implementing the Traveller Health Strategy;
- ensuring that all minority ethnic groups, including those who are asylum-seekers, can access training opportunities relevant to their needs and active supports to assist their integration into the labour market;
- ensuring that ethnic minority groups have access to adequate housing/accommodation, avoiding their marginalisation or ghettoisation in one part of a city and re-examining the barriers to integration and the break up of family networks as a result of the 'dispersal' and 'direct provision' systems;
- imposing sanctions on local authorities that do not make sufficient progress under the Traveller Accommodation Programme;
- developing arts policies and programmes that support and

promote the cultural traditions of minority ethnic groups and foster intercultural approaches;

- further developing the support for community development projects with ethnic minority groups, the networking of ethnic minority groups and their involvement in social partnership processes;
- building a focus on minority ethnic groups and inter-agency cooperation at local level through the plans being developed by City and County Development Boards, the work of local development partnerships, the Integrated Services Initiative and the Rapid initiative in the most disadvantaged communities;
- ensuring the availability of translation services to the Gardaí to enable the most vulnerable to have access to protection, particularly in relation to racist attacks.

Conclusion

In conclusion, it is worth reiterating that, although we currently do not have hard data, minority ethnic groups are almost certainly at higher risk of poverty than the population as a whole. The number of people belonging to ethnic minority groups coming in to Ireland will almost inevitably increase over the coming years. While this will be a positive and permanent change that will lead to a more culturally rich and diverse society, there is also a danger that many of those coming here will be at great risk of poverty. This will certainly be the case if we do nothing now to prevent it. We cannot afford to sit back and wait for this to happen and then try to pick up the pieces. We should take steps now to prevent it. This will require developing proactive strategies to challenge racist attitudes in society and to promote cultural/ethnic awareness and social solidarity. It will also involve developing better targeted supports and services for immigrants, refugees and asylum-seekers. We must do likewise for minority ethnic groups already here. Ultimately, the aim of policy should be to eliminate both racism and poverty completely. However, while we are working towards this we should at least ensure that the risk of poverty for someone from an ethnic minority is no higher than for someone from the majority population and that they are not at greater risk of exclusion because of racism.

Notes

1   The most recent research evidence, a special Eurobarometer survey carried out for the European Commission by the European Centre on Racism and Xenophobia, found that almost one fifth of people in Ireland find the presence of people from another nationality disturbing in their daily lives and almost a third (30 per cent) believe immigrants are more often involved in crime than are non-immigrants.

2   *The Role of Community Development in Tackling Poverty,* Combat Poverty Agency, Dublin, 2000

3   See *Developing an Anti-Racism Dimension to the National Anti-Poverty Strategy Poverty Proofing Guidelines: Case Studies to Inform Implementation,* prepared by the the National Consultative Committee on Racism and Interculturalism, December 1999, for ideas on how this might best be done.

The Potential of
Public Awareness Programmes

Kensika Monshengwo

THE AIM OF THIS CHAPTER is to consider the contribution that
national public awareness programmes can make to addressing
racism; it is presented here as a contribution to the emerging
methodologies, at international level, concerning the planning,
implementation and review of such programmes. It is of
particular relevance to Ireland where a national anti-racism
public awareness programme is being developed.

Drawing comparisons with the experience of other
countries in undertaking public awareness programmes is not a
straightforward task. No one country is precisely analogous
with another, and as one would expect, different countries have
adopted different approaches to developing such programmes.
A further difficulty in making such comparisons with other
countries is that despite significant resources being applied to
public awareness programmes, few are comprehensively
evaluated. This makes it difficult to assess the methodologies,
outcomes and impact of such programmes.

International case studies from other countries are,
therefore, best viewed as providing ideas and insights, rather
than being considered as templates for replication. Two
countries that have been to the forefront in developing national
awareness programmes are Canada and Australia.

Canada

Each year since 1989 the Department of Canadian Heritage, through its Multiculturalism Program Directorate, implements an awareness programme that coincides with 21st March, International Day Against Racism. The campaign focuses on young people and the role of education in highlighting racism and promoting a multicultural Canada. Activities are organised at national, regional and local level. The particular emphasis on community-based approaches – involving a range of government and non-government partners – has promoted a broad sense of ownership of the aims of the day.

One of the key strengths of the Canadian approach to developing public awareness programmes such as 21st March is that they are seen to be an integral part of a broader framework of policies to promote a more multicultural Canada. In 1988 the Canadian Parliament enacted legislation for promoting a more inclusive and pluralist society known as the Multiculturalism Act. The Act takes the innovative approach of declaring it to be the policy of the Government of Canada to:

- recognise and promote the understanding that multi-culturalism reflects the cultural and racial diversity of Canadian society and to acknowledge the freedom of all members of Canadian society to preserve, enhance and share their cultural heritage
- promote the full and equitable participation of individuals and communities of all origins in the continuing evolution and shaping of all aspects of Canadian society and to assist them in the elimination of any barrier to such participation
- ensure that all individuals receive equal treatment and equal protection under the law while respecting and valuing diversity
- encourage and assist the social, cultural, economic and

political instructions of Canada to be both respectful and inclusive of Canada's multicultural character

The evaluation of the 21st March initiative in Canada points to the strengths and weaknesses in the programme. In particular, the evaluation points to the need for such programmes to focus on changing behaviours and practices as well as changing attitudes. The evaluations further point to the importance of a long-term approach, based on consistency of message and imagery, and the importance of key messages being repeated and reinforced over a period of time. The evaluation emphasises the importance of broad participation and ownership of such programmes by key stakeholders, such as community and voluntary groups, regional authorities, trade union, employer and church organisations

Australia

In Australia, the Department of Immigration and Multicultural Affairs initiated the 'Living in Harmony Initiative' in 1998. The initiative was linked to debate in Australia about the treatment of refugees, asylum-seekers and Aboriginals within Australia.

The Living in Harmony Initiative provides community groups and non-governmental organisations with the funding to conduct their own activities at a regional and local level. It also recognises the 21st of March as 'National Harmony Day'. Different sectors of society, including community groups, businesses and government bodies, are encouraged to collaborate and mark the day with different activities.

To date, the programme has not been formally evaluated, but there are indications that while community groups have welcomed the resources to participate in the programme, there is ongoing concern about the limited leadership provided by central government involvement. Some groups have been critical of the perception that high-level political leadership and support for the programme has been modest and the profile and status of the programme have suffered accordingly.

The initiative was also undermined somewhat by a significant delay between the announcement to proceed with the initiative and its actual implementation, resulting in the perception that the programme was not a central priority for the government, a perception that was highlighted by other political parties and the media in Australia.

Issues arising for policy in Ireland

These two case studies provide a number of insights that have relevance to developing an anti-racism programme in Ireland, including:

- the benefits of developing a public awareness programme as an integral part of a wider framework of policies to address racism
- the need for high level and sustained political support as an essential element in the success of the programme
- the need to seek cross-party political support for such a programme
- the overall advantages accruing from planning and implementing the programme in partnership with a wide range of 'stakeholders', such as community groups, and social partners
- the importance of resourcing other sectors to participate and to feel ownership of the programme
- the need to send consistent and reinforced key messages about the programme
- the importance of reviewing and evaluating public awareness programmes
- public awareness programmes should seek to be ambitious and to create the conditions for changes in behaviour, practice and policy as well as changes in attitude

- the need to ensure that the programme is not undermined
  by significant delays

The National Consultative Committee on Racism and
Interculturalism (NCCRI) drew up an evaluation for a national
anti-racism public awareness programme in Ireland. The
evaluation, which was approved by the Irish Government in
October 2000, stresses that if a public awareness programme in
Ireland is to be successful, it will require the mobilisation of a
wide range of sectors, including those involved in the
education system, the media, the community and voluntary
sectors, the business sector, statutory bodies, political parties
and other key groups with a leadership role in Irish society.

Following the cabinet decision to approve the NCCRI
evaluation of the programme, a high-level steering group was
established to work with the Equal Status Division of the
Department of Justice, Equality and Law Reform to implement
the programme. A budget of £4.5million was allocated over
three years.

If the programme is to be judged as successful, the NCCRI
evaluation contends that there must be evidence of significant
and sustainable impact from the programme, including impact
on public policy. Different sectors of society must be involved
and encouraged to work together wherever possible. The
campaign should seek to rise above party political concerns and
the support of party leaders for the programme should be
sought. The evaluation contends that it is essential that
minority ethnic groups participate in the programme. It also
seeks to ensure that the implementation of the different aspects
of the programme generates a multiplicity of effects. The
programme should also seek to build on the work of existing
initiatives such as the March 21st programme coordinated by
the NCCRI and the Equality Commission (NI) and the Racism

in the Workplace Week coordinated by the Equality Authority, Irish Congress of Trade Unionists, Irish Business Employers Confederation, and the Construction Industry Federation.

Areas of intervention

The following have been identified as some of the key areas of intervention advocated for the anti-racism awareness programmes in Ireland.

Education

In its submission to the Expert Advisory Group on the Content and Duration of Post-Primary Teacher Education, the NCCRI highlighted the potential of Education Policies in promoting an inclusive society: 'Education policy and programmes could contribute to the fight against racism and this potential should be utilised.'[1]

An anti-racist and intercultural education is essential to the development of an equitable and more inclusive society, where cultural diversity is valued and respected. Besides, the White Paper on Adult Education includes interculturalism as one of the core principles that should underpin approaches to developing adult education and states that there is a 'need to frame educational policy and practice in the context of serving a diverse population as opposed to a uniform one, and the development of curricula, materials, training and in-service, modes of assessment and delivery methods which accepts such diversity as the norm.'[2]

The education system, formal and informal, has in the past instilled prejudices and racism in its curricula and materials. The promotion of different perspectives in history teaching is vital to challenge prejudices and stereotypes. Many history books, for instance, commence African history with the story of slavery followed by colonisation and end with the conditions of the poor third world countries. Such an abridged version of African history contributes to patronising attitudes to Africans and doesn't encourage Irish children to see Africans as their equals.

Since one learns how to be racist, one can also learn how not to be. A key challenge for the forthcoming awareness programme should be to help create the conditions where existing barriers to equality and interculturalism in the education system can be overcome. Examples of concrete interventions might be the development of specific guidelines and materials for schools.

As part of the preparations for the public awareness programme the NCCRI in partnership with the Equality Commission for Northern Ireland, published a resource pack available to all schools in Ireland, North and South (www.nccri.com).

The media

'We live in a society dominated by the media. They influence attitudes, prejudices and people's capacity to act.'[3]

The media have made a significant contribution to highlighting racism in Ireland and promoting a more inclusive society. However, it has also been recognised that the media can be a source of prejudice and racism.

As a matter of fact, the treatment of the refugee issue by the Irish media influenced public opinion negatively and dangerously in relation to refugees and asylum-seekers in particular, and foreigners in general.[4] These concerns have been voiced by a wide range of people, including those working directly in the media, who have advocated a need to raise awareness about the way minority ethnic groups are sometimes depicted. The media needs to be directly involved in the public awareness programme, in a supportive way as well as simply as a conveyor of messages. Increasing the number of journalists from minority ethnic backgrounds and supporting minority ethnic media providers could also be important outcomes from the public awareness programme.

Statutory bodies
As well as being aware of the issues around racism, the awareness programme needs to assist the statutory sector to acquire the necessary skills to understand and meet the challenge associated with an emerging multi-ethnic society.

Some of the interventions that could be highlighted through the programme could include statutory bodies adopting policies and action plans to undertake anti-racism training and to promote interculturalism. The myths and labels attached to minority ethnic groups need to be dismantled; those guilty of racism and other forms of discrimination should be prosecuted; the systemic causes of inequality must be challenged. In order to transform society as a whole, equality and anti-racism practices should become embedded in the ethos of the different statutory bodies as part of a broader equality framework.

The role of civil society
Civil society, in particular the community and voluntary sector and other social partner organisations, has contributed significantly to the emergence of strategies to address racism at European and national level and should have a key role to play in the development of a national anti-racism public awareness programme

The leadership from civil society in addressing racism has been a consistent feature of policy development across Europe and within Ireland. The role of Non-Governmental Organisations has also been recognised at a global level and is a key feature of the World Conference on Racism.

The role of NGOs can include:

- campaigning and lobbying for stronger government action to address racism
- participating in partnership initiatives to address racism
- facilitating the participation of minority ethnic groups in measures to address racism
- raising public awareness
- highlighting the experience of groups that experience racism

The NGO sector needs to be adequately resourced to play an active role in the public awareness programme.

Conclusion
Drawing on the outcomes from the NCCRI evaluation, including the research from other countries, it is clear that a public awareness programme in Ireland should:

- be developed as one element of an integrated government plan to combat racism
- seek to gain widespread support from key sectors, including the statutory sector, the social partners and civil society
- be implemented by a range of different bodies, with central coordination

The way that the programme in Ireland is implemented will be the key to its success; in particular it is important that the programme is widely perceived as being concerned with public awareness rather than public relations. It is particularly appropriate that the launch of the national public awareness programme in Ireland coincides with the period following the World Conference on Racism and follows Ireland's ratification of the International Convention on the Elimination of all forms of Racial Discrimination.

Notes

1   NCCRI, Submission to the Expert Advisory Group on the Content and Duration of Post-Primary Teacher Education.

2   White Paper on Adult Education – *Learning for Life Department of Education and Science,* July 2000, p. 13.

3   Winkler, B. Dr, 'European Media Conference – Why?' in *Cultural Diversity – Against Racism,* Vienna: European Monitoring Centre on Racism and Xenophobia, 1999, p.11.

4   Pollak, A., 'An invitation to racism? Irish daily newspaper coverage of the refugee issue', in *Media in Ireland: the research for ethical journalism,* ed. Damien Kiberd, Dublin: Open Air, 1999, p. 34.

THE ROLE OF CHURCHES

Fr Donal O'Mahony OFM Cap

Introduction

THERE ARE MANY DIFFERENT forms of racism and racial prejudices that underlie racist behaviour. For example, ethnocentricity is a widespread attitude whereby a people or nation has a natural tendency to defend its identity by denigrating that of others. While such behaviour may respond to an instinctive need to protect the values, beliefs and customs of one's own community, we need to be reminded that the rejection of differences can lead to a form of cultural annihilation, which sociologists have called 'ethnocide'. Balance is required here.

Then there is social racism, which applies not only towards groups in terms of their hereditary physical traits, but by extension to all persons whose ethnic origins, language, religion or customs make them appear different. The Traveller community in Irish society is an obvious example.

A new and as yet unknown form of racism is in danger of making its appearance through the techniques of artificial procreation and genetic manipulation. In the hands of abusive and irresponsible people such techniques might be used to 'produce' human beings selected according to racial criteria or any other characteristic giving rise to a resurgence of 'eugenic racism', the misdeeds of which the world has already experienced.

However, for the purpose of this chapter our focus will be particularly on issues related to resident foreigners, refugees and asylum-seekers.

In the first section, I will be asking if the time is now ripe for Churches to take the wider cosmic story more into account in religious education when teaching about how humans fit into the world. For this may well be a partial solution to the growing world-wide problem of asylum-seekers, refugees and the subsequent manifestations of racism. I believe there is a need today to go back beyond religion, beyond the advent of the human race, to look anew at planet earth upon which all life depends. This does not mean, of course, that the Churches should play down or ignore the unique position of the human person as a creature of God. Nor does it imply that they should stop examining other root causes that lie behind the problems faced by asylum-seekers and refugees, including racism, the disregard for the principle of the equal dignity of all persons, the phenomenon of fear, the existence of war, the violation of human rights, the negative consequences of dictatorships and systems of social oppression, the weakening of the nation-state and so on. But for the longer term view, I believe it is time to bring to an end a virtual theological and pastoral silence about the significance and implications for the everyday mortal on the street concerning his/her self-understanding in our contemporary cosmos. A broader canvas with an ecologically sensitive brush may help the Churches respond more comprehensively to the enormous population displacements and racist attitudes prevalent today.

The second section will be less theoretical. I will look at very positive institutional responses being made by the Irish Churches to the question of asylum-seekers, refugees and the

combatting of racist attitudes. In the third section, by way of
conclusion, I will make some comments on how the whole
Church as the people of God can make a more telling and
coordinated response in the context of their daily lives.

An earth perspective

Holding a view or taking an action that is intended to diminish
or exclude persons because of their ethnicity, colour or place of
origin is something abhorrently evil. It is the worst form of
human rejection because it is connected innately to a person's
biological being. It is also, arguably, the greatest 'NO!' that any
free person can say to God, the Creator of heaven and earth.
Other forms of discrimination based on status, wealth,
education or religious affiliation need to be challenged of
course, but rejecting persons because of something that is
intrinsic to their being places this form of discrimination into a
totally different league. We term it 'racism'. Racism, whether it
be institutional or otherwise, is an expression of a total
rejection of what it means to be a person. From a moral
perspective, racism is a sin that cries out to heaven and is
blasphemy to the Creator. Today in Ireland, some asylum-
seekers and refugees are subjected to various forms of
discrimination and racist slurs. This must rightly be a major
concern for all the Churches.

My own understanding of the vulnerability of refugees goes
back many years. There were many occasions relating to my
work at that time, when I would visit refugee camps in different
parts of the world. For example, I recall visiting a Christian
Palestinians refugee camp in Beiruit. They were hated and
rejected by many in the local population, and seen as
'dangerous' by most Moslems. But the truth was that these
refugees were living in fear for their lives. Some Palestinian
men who belonged to the camp acted as armed defenders at the

entry to the camp. Inside, I listened to their horrific stories and learned how they were struggling to survive and retain some glimmer of hope. They lived in shocking, inhuman conditions. Their huts were literally laid out in the form of a maze to make it difficult for attackers to gain entry; or, if by chance they succeeded in getting in, they would find it next to impossible to find their way out.

What remains most in my memory was the sense of abandonment and the total experience of isolation that the refugees felt. The loss of home, family and friends. The spiritual poverty of being homeless, stateless and that empty feeling of not belonging anywhere. It is impossible to describe such feelings adequately. But later on I would encounter the very same in other refugee centres. I remember visiting a refugee camp in Slovenia at the height of the fighting in former Yugoslavia. In this camp there were many Moslems and Christians, mostly women and children, living side by side but mutually afraid and distrustful of each other. What was common to them all, however, was a shared anxiety and worry about husbands, fathers, sons fighting to the death within a half-day's journey of the camp.

How can such ethnic hatreds exist? As a Church person in Ireland, I have often reflected upon this question. As part of this reflection I have come to the conclusion that one of the long term goals of the Churches must be to re-evaluate the human person in the context of the modern-day understanding of our evolution and origins. The foundation for such reasoning is based on a solid axiom:

A phenomenon remains unexplainable as long as the range of the observation is not wide enough to include the context in which the phenomenon occurs.

For too long we have radically separated human beings from the rest of creation. This anthropocentric emphasis has had the

effect of narrowing possibilities for people to cultivate deep
earth-human relationships. So long as we believe that we are
separate from and superior to the rest of nature, individualism
and 'tribal' self-centeredness – as well as a loss of overall
psychological cohesion among different ethnic groups – will
continue. Our too human-centered theology actively
contributes to a collective egotism that nurtures fear,
discrimination, violence and, as a consequence, a growth in
racism, asylum-seekers and refugees.

A great number of physicists today now support, in a
general way, the Christian belief that the universe is created as
a communion. A communion, it may be added, which reflects
in some way the communion of the Blessed Trinity in whose
image creation was made.[1]

Suffice, however, to say that at the moment it is no longer
uncomfortable for some theologians and many scientists to
declare that all matter in the world 'aspires' towards life, life
towards self-consciousness and self-consciousness towards
universal communion. It is within this perspective that I believe
the Churches should be speaking to our contemporary world.
This is how creation, incarnation and redemption could be
presented. 'For in Christ all the fullness of God was pleased to
dwell, and through him God was pleased to reconcile to himself
all things, whether on earth or in heaven, by making peace
through his blood, shed on the Cross' (Coll.1:19-20). With this
conviction, our human species might become a little more
humble, a little less discriminatory and hopefully less violent.
For it is fair to say that if humans are unmindful of the earth,
from which they were born and by which they are nourished
and healed, they will be unmindful of one another.

As humans we are probably descendants not only of a
primitive form of man and woman (*homo erectus*), not only of
monkeys and bacteria but also of the stars and the galaxies. To

present the new scientific story of our universe very briefly: our world is made up of the debris of stars that existed earlier in the history of the universe. These early stars were essentially nuclear reactors, building up chemicals such as carbon that are indispensable for life. Some of these stars exploded, scattering the debris into space. The process took a few billion years. Eventually, some of the debris collected to form the earth. Primitive forms of life developed. But it took more than 4 billion years more for humans to emerge. In a purely biological sense there is a continuous chain between homo sapiens and other animals – we still share more than 98 per cent of our genes with chimpanzees.[2] The same elements of which our bodies are composed, are those that billions of years ago brought the universe into being. We can say that matter, life and consciousness form one single history of evolution. It has taken the full course of the evolution of the universe, 12 billion years, of the earth, 4.5 billion years of humanity (homo habilis, about 3 million years), to acquire the fragile freedom that today confers on humans the ability to recognise and respect that we, and all of nature, belong to the same ancestral tree. Wherefore this ethnic hatred?

This, then, is the wider perspective that we are proposing. The need to contextualise the human person in a manner that is at once faithful to the Christian tradition and the twentieth-century sciences. It is a challenge to the current thinking of the Churches.

More specifically, how might this wider perspective help counter the problems of refugees and racist attitudes in Ireland?

At least in the three following ways:

• it will provide the necessary larger backdrop upon which to reflect on the principle of unity in all human relationships. It

would be an antidote to exclusion. 'We are dust – 'star dust'
as Australian theologian, Denis Edwards states – and 'into
dust we shall return' as the Lenten liturgy of Ash
Wednesday reminds us. The great medieval saint, Francis of
Assisi, responded well to such cosmic wholeness. He sang
the praises of unity. He ignored the philosophical,
hierarchical structure of being. He had one simple vision: all
beings (human and non-human alike) share creaturehood
under the one Creator. His refusal to violate this
'ontological relationship' has made him a universally loved
saint. With this vision, Francis would not, could not exclude
anyone. It provided him with a very special relationship to
the powerless, to minority groups, and to all of nature. He
did more than simply praise God for all his creatures, he
fraternised with them all. And this was new. Humans, the
wind and the ocean, the animals and the birds became his
brothers and sisters. It is within that context that the
Churches might successfully respond to the evil of
discrimination and racism.

- the evolutionary 'earth perspective' also indicates that we
  humans are, most probably, all originally African. About
  three million years ago, the population of the world was
  150,000 humans, all living in a small corner of Africa. Two
  million years ago there were several million humans. Ten
  thousand years ago there were ten to twenty million
  humans. Two hundred years ago there were a billion
  humans. Today, there are approximately six billion humans.
  So truly there is no such thing as different races. The
  differences that exist are to be found only in the level of
  tissues, cells, molecules – distinctions that are quite
  insignificant. Knowledge of these facts alone should incite
  us to think and act fraternally and make racist attitudes look
  as unintelligent and stupid as they are.

- the lack of a cosmic perspective is contributing to the ecological destruction of the earth, which, in turn, is partly responsible for the forcible uprooting of millions of humans from their own countries to be transplanted into areas of the world unfamiliar, and often climatically and culturally unsuitable for them and their families. We do not often think enough of the great number of asylum-seekers and refugees of the world as really being the victims of a widespread ecological degradation. A degradation that has its roots in a lack of respect and appreciation for the earth as well as some ill-founded efforts by Third World countries in responding and aping the voracious greed of international capitalism.

The United Nations has made it clear that the ecological strain placed on the earth is both the cause and an effect of political tension and military conflicts, which in turn is responsible for the increase of the number of refugees in today's world, reckoned to be close on 50 million. For example, a report of the UN World Commission on Environment and Development fourteen years ago stated that there is a growing concern by the international community about the emerging phenomenon of 'environmental refugees'. It may appear, at first sight, that the immediate cause of any mass movement of refugees is political upheaval and military violence. But the underlying cause for this upheaval and military violence is often due to the deterioration of the natural resource bases and the capacity to support the population in these countries.

The UN Report further refers to places like the Horn of Africa to illustrate what they mean; when the first major drought and famine struck the nation of Ethiopia, it was discovered that the hunger and human misery were caused more by years of overuse of the soil in the Ethiopian highlands

and the resultant erosion, than by the drought. The Ethiopian
Relief and Rehabilitation Commission later declared that 'the
primary cause of the famine was not the drought which was of
unprecedented severity, but a combination of long-continued
bad land use and steadily increased human and stock
populations over decades'.[3] It has been a similar experience in
many other parts of the world.

Paradoxically, the enormous outflow of refugees and
asylum-seekers reluctantly compelled to leave their own
culture and familiar surroundings are often now, unwittingly,
participants in the very First World policies that were
responsible for forcing them to leave their country in the first
place. Many refugees, without being aware of it, contribute to
the environmentally-related military and political havoc of
their home countries. Saddest of all, perhaps, is the fact that,
again through no fault of their own, the refugees are the
occasion for the heightening of interstate tensions. And when
(if) they come to Europe, the US or other wealthy regions of
the world, they easily become subject to racists slurs, physical
abuse and are made to feel unwelcome.

In summary, the three points we have made about refugees,
asylum-seekers and racism within an 'earth perspective' form a
challenge to the Churches to look deeper than the usual
anthropocentric response. A fundamental question the
Churches have to ask today is: what practical efforts are needed
to harmonise the world of nature and the community of
peoples with national economies? We may all rue the day if we
choose to leave out the evolutionary and ecological dimensions
of this question. Solidarity is required, not only to unite
refugees and asylum-seekers with the human family, but also to
unite the whole human family and planet earth. The Churches
in Ireland need to think, talk and act out the implications of
being part of a 'cosmic fraternity'.

How the institutional Christian Churches in Ireland are responding to the asylum-seekers, refugees and racism
Racist ideologies and behaviour are long-standing: they are rooted in the reality of sin from the very beginning of humanity, as we can see in the biblical accounts of Cain and Abel as well as in that of the Tower of Babel.

The Church would say that racial prejudice, in the strict sense of the word, is a belief in a biologically determined superiority of ones own race or ethnic group with respect to others. In this sense it can be distinguished from unjust, discriminatory behaviour. The Greeks, for example, were convinced of the cultural superiority of their civilization, but they did not consider the 'barbarians' inferior because of innate biological reasons. That, of course, did not justify them for making them slaves when captured, at their masters' disposal.

An appalling manifestation of racism in modern times was the ideology of Hitler. Nazism was a racist ideology that aimed at the physical elimination of those 'races' it deemed 'inferior', and so became responsible for one of the greatest genocides in history. And as can easily happen, the step from racism to eugenics was quickly taken.

Today, racism has not disappeared from our planet. In the Irish context, while it may seem that segregation based on racial theories is not part of our culture, there are manifestations of spontaneous racist attitudes and actions which amount to exclusion and non-acceptance of diversity. We see this on the streets when certain groups of persons whose physical appearance or ethnic, cultural or religious characteristics are interpreted as innately different and so justifying discriminatory practices and even aggressivity in their regard.

The Churches have responded very positively to the current refugee situation in Ireland. They have been outspoken about the search for just and lasting solutions to what John Paul II has called 'perhaps the greatest tragedy of all the human tragedies of our time'. The Catholic Church has set up a Refugee Project under the Irish Bishops' Conference to inform the public and monitor the asylum-seeker/refugee situation in Ireland. This Refugee Project is ecumenically engaged with many other Churches in its work. They also issue information bulletins and arrange inter-Church meetings on a regular basis.

At Christmas 1999 a statement was issued by the Catholic Bishops called 'Receiving the Stranger'; in this statement, the bishops made it clear that 'our faith leaves no room for double-think on the matter of racism and hatred for foreigners (xenophobia). We have to avoid racist behaviour ourselves and oppose it wherever it arises: insulting graffiti, threatening phone calls, verbal abuse, racially motivated intimidation or violence, discrimination in accommodation, biased or misleading media coverage: such behaviour is culpable and may have untold consequences for already vulnerable individuals.'

In another statement on 26th April 2000, the bishops called for regularisation of asylum-seekers. They drew attention to the existence of two groups – a growing backlog of asylum-seekers whose applications have not been processed, and a second group whose applications have been processed and rejected but who, for various reasons, have not yet been asked to leave the country. They suggested that regularisation could be effected by granting refugee status on a bloc-basis to all who applied for asylum by a given date; giving asylum-seekers who applied for asylum by a certain date the alternative of applying for immigrant worker status for a stated period; and granting humanitarian leave to remain in the country. Bishop Laurence Ryan (President of the Irish Commission for Justice and Peace), Bishop John Kirby (Chairperson of Trocaire), Bishop Jim Moriarty (President of the Council for Social Welfare) and

Bishop Fiachra Ó Ceallaigh, OFM (Chairperson of the Irish Bishops' Refugee Project) concluded by issuing a strong public appeal: 'At this juncture in our national social and economic development we have, as always, a choice. We can choose to turn more inwards on ourselves, or we can choose to create a more welcoming, inclusive society, prepared to share some of its increasing wealth and opportunities with others, just as in the past other countries were prepared to give a place to Irish people fleeing persecution or poverty in their own country. The choice should be in favour of inclusiveness...'

In December 2000, an extensive briefing document on behalf of the Committee on Asylum-Seekers and Refugees of the Irish Catholic Bishops' Conference was issued. It was called 'Pre-Emptive Exclusion of Asylum-Seekers? Disturbing Evidence of a New Policy'. In this document, they point out that from the beginning of July 2000 up to 19th November 2000 there had been a consistent pattern of arrival of asylum-seekers (averaging between one hundred and forty and two hundred per month) coming from Cherbourg and landing in Rosslare, as measured by referrals to the South Eastern Health Board. But between 20th November and 5th December of the same year not one asylum-seeker was referred to the Health Board. So, the Bishops asked, have the Irish immigration authorities adopted a new practice and/or policy of pre-emptive exclusion of asylum-seekers travelling on the Rosslare-Cherbourg route? If so, the object of such a policy would appear to be to prevent potential asylum-seekers from actually making an application for asylum in Ireland by the simple expedient of preventing them from disembarking in the first place. The bishops concluded that such a policy would make 'illegal trafficking more profitable, even apart from the question of legality and compliance with a state's international human rights and humanitarian obligations.'

Financially, all Churches and many religious orders generously assist many voluntary lay groups working on the ground with asylum-seekers and refugees, e.g. NASC based in Cork, or, for example the Vincentian Centre in Dublin. In addition, the Refugee Project has also sought information from every religious congregation in Ireland. On 17th April 2000, they issued a letter to all Congregations in the country about the possible existence of accommodation and properties that might prove helpful to the government in assisting asylum-seekers and refugees. The response was generous.

The Churches' Peace Education Programme published an excellent biblical perspective on racism, immigration, asylum and cross-community issues that schools and small working groups all over Ireland have found most helpful.[4] The Refugee Project of the Irish Bishops' Conference issues a regular newsletter, circulated widely, called *Sanctuary*. It reports on issues pertaining to 'Asylum and Refugee Matters from a Religious Perspective'. Finally, the Irish Commission for Justice and Peace under the Catholic Bishop's Conference, prepared a very substantive Asylum-Seeker/Refugee Information Pack, which has received wide praise.

In the context of our daily lives

So what then should the priorities be for God's believing community in Ireland today? Because homelessness is at the heart of the refugee experience, hospitality should be at the heart of the Church's mission. A real, warm welcome is what most refugees most need. And this is in harmony with recurring themes of the Bible. Whether the guest arrives at the expected time or not – and the latter is more common – we are invited to keep our lamps burning and watch faithfully and patiently (Mt 25:1-13; Lk 12:35). The quality of our welcome to the stranger – as a messenger from God – is the key criterion for our authentic faithfulness to God.[5]

The Irish Churches need to work together with ecumenical endeavour. The care of refugees in Ireland offers a very special opportunity for Churches to contact and give practical help to persons of other faiths such as Muslims, Hindus, Buddhists or Taoist. It is not enough for the people of God's Church to agree with concepts such as inclusivity and the doctrine of the unity of all in God. People must witness their faith by actions. We are asked to counter racists remarks and defend victims of racism whenever and wherever it occurs. As Scripture reminds us: 'If one of the brothers or one of the sisters is in need of clothes and has not enough food to live on, and one of you says to them, 'I wish you well; keep yourself warm and eat plenty', without giving them the necessities of life, then what good is that? Faith is like that: if good works do not go with it, it is quite dead' (Jm 2:15-17).

Ultimately, racial prejudice will not be uprooted by external laws or by defending victims of racism. To overcome discrimination, God's people must interiorise the values that inspire just laws and live out, in their day-to-day lives, the conviction of the equal dignity of all. To succeed in doing this there needs to be a strengthening of spiritual convictions regarding respect for others. Priests, teachers and catechists need to give emphasis to the true teaching of Scripture and to the tradition of the origin of all people in God; the final destiny of all created beings is the Kingdom of God.

In Ireland today, many of the asylum-seekers and refugees are still in shock. They carry a deep sense of loss and grief. Some are humiliated, afraid, anxious, depressed, fearful and disoriented. Many feel wronged. The tension is great. Only recently, a very tense situation occurred for 170 asylum-seekers in 'direct provision' in Cork. The asylum-seekers were asked to move out (because of fire regulations), with less than twenty-four hour notice, to be dispersed to various parts of the city and county. Their angry reaction was due to their fear of being deported. Refugees are a people living on the edge and so are often suspicious. So welcome the refugee as she or he passes through your parish or diocese. Our practical commitment to refugees and asylum-seekers should become a test of the authenticity of our faith. In fact, under God, they may be the chosen human instruments of renewing and strengthening our faith.

Notes

1 For a flavour of the religious views of scientists under one cover see *Cosmos, Bios, Theos*, eds Henry Margenau and Roy Varghese, Open Court, La Salle, Illinois (1992). It gives the religious views of seventy contemporary scientists on their understanding of reality. More than twenty of those interviewed are Nobel Prize winners.

2 For further insights into the remarkable story of the integrity of all creation, read, for example, *The New Cosmology*, Thomas Berry, Twenty-third Publications (1987); *Theology and Scientific Knowledge*, Christopher Mooney, SJ, University of Notre Dame Press (1997); *Religion in an Age of Science*, Ian Barbour, Harper and Rowe, San Francisco (1990); *Gaia Connections*, Alan Miller, Rowman and Littlefield (1991); *The Universe is a Green Dragon*, Brian Swimme, Bear & Co. (1988); *Designer Universe*, John Wright, Monarch Publications, Broadway House, East Sussex (1994); *Origins*, Hubert Reeves, Joel De Rosnay, Yves Coppens and Dominique Simonnet, Arcade Publishing Inc., NY (1998); *Jesus and the Cosmos*, Denis Edwards, Paulist Press, New Jersey (1991).

3 *Our Common Future*, World Commission on Environment and Development, Oxford University Press (1987).

4 *What the Bible Says About the Stranger*, Kieran J. O'Mahony, OSA. Churches' Peace Education Programme (1999). Available from Irish Commission for Justice and Peace, 169 Booterstown Avenue, Blackrock, Co. Dublin.

5 A most helpful book for the layperson is *Refugees and Forcibly Displaced People* (Veritas, 2000), Mark Raper, SJ, and Amaya Valcarcel.

LEGAL AND INSTITUTIONAL RESPONSES

Niall Crowley

Introduction

NOSTALGIC AND SELF-INDULGENT perspectives of Ireland as 'Ireland of the Welcomes' have, in recent times, foundered on the experience of multi-ethnic Ireland. 'Nostalgic and self-indulgent' might appear a harsh description to attribute to such perspectives. Yet, while it is only recently that such perspectives have foundered, Ireland has been multi-ethnic for many generations. The mythical 'Ireland of the Welcomes' merely served a denial of racism as a very unacceptable dimension to our make-up as a society.

We do not yet deal well with difference. We never have. Difference is a source of concern rather than of celebration and excitement. Difference is a threat rather than a challenge full of potential. Difference is about deviance rather than choice and creativity. This has not just applied to minority ethnic groups. It has applied across differences of gender, religion, disability, age and sexual orientation, among others.

Racism has been constructed around cultural difference. A society free from racism must be the goal. However, this must be more than a society that condemns physical and verbal abuse while remaining a place where black and minority ethnic people should know their position and be grateful for the

tolerance demonstrated. It must be more than a society that
condemns discrimination while failing to accommodate
cultural difference in the way we organise our business.

In this way we raise our ambitions to seek an intercultural
society. This would be a society where black and minority
ethnic people have a sense of belonging and a sense of
ownership – a society that black and minority ethnic people can
identify with without diminishing anybody's ethnic identity.
There is a need for creativity to envision how such a society
might be organised. Irish society has a long way to go in
realising such a vision and we need an adequate institutional
framework to guide us along the way. This guidance will need
to secure a new approach to cultural difference.

We need to go beyond acknowledging or tolerating cultural
difference to actively according positive value to this difference.
We need to develop a capacity to identify the practical
implications of cultural difference and to create arenas where
these can be negotiated into policy and provision. Then, of
course, we need to deliver on this negotiation by
accommodating cultural diversity in the way we do business as
a society.

An institutional framework capable of such an approach is
required at national and local levels. It is also required within
individual institutions. It involves agenda-setting and
participation, mainstreaming and targeting, and rights and
institutions to drive forward such rights.

Agenda-setting and participation
The Report of the Task Force on the Travelling Community
provides a valuable model in relation to agenda-setting and
participation. It is the first official document that sets out to
envision what an intercultural society might look like. It
involves the according of value to cultural difference, the

identification of the practical implications of this difference, and a negotiation of how best to incorporate these into policy making and service provision.

The Task Force reported in 1995. Its second chapter is an exploration of cultural difference as it relates to Travellers and of the value to be accorded to this. It found that:

> The important contribution of cultural diversity to the well-being of a society should also be acknowledged. Cultural diversity provides a society with a broader range of perspectives and frames of reference. Cultural diversity in a context of mutual respect means that communities with different cultures can provide different approaches and solutions to common problems.

It concludes by recommending 'that the distinct culture and identity of the Traveller Community be recognised and taken into account'. It went on to trace this recommendation out in terms of its relevance to policy and provision in the areas of accommodation, health, education, training and economic development.

The Task Force was a negotiating arena that brought together all relevant interests. Travellers and Traveller organisations were engaged in a negotiation with politicians, Government Departments, and local authorities. The effective participation of Travellers and Traveller organisations was key to real negotiation. Effective participation was rooted in a background of high levels of organisation within the Traveller community with space and capacity to tease out and agree the agendas to be brought to the negotiating table.

The Task Force recommendations provide a blueprint for progress. Significant challenges remain, however, to secure their realisation. An institutional infrastructure has been developed, based on the participation of Travellers and Traveller organisations, to drive the implementation of the recommendations. However, progress in implementation has been slow. The Task Force does provide a model that could usefully be deployed across other minority ethnic groups in Irish society. This would require the formation of appropriate arenas of negotiation, alongside investment, in assisting greater levels of organisation within these communities.

Participation is central to effective agenda setting. However, communities need resources to organise, to identify their shared needs and aspirations and to articulate these as part of the building of an intercultural society. This process is at a very early stage in many minority ethnic communities. It is hampered by small numbers, dispersal, lack of resources and the vulnerable situation many members of these communities are experiencing. Investment and effort is required to change this and to create the necessary context for agenda setting.

Participation needs to go beyond time-limited, agenda-setting Task Forces. It needs to go beyond an institutional infrastructure to implement recommendations made. It needs to be an element of governance, of how we make decisions as a society. Social partnership in Ireland reflects a significant evolution of governance to combine representative and participate models. The National Economic and Social Council, the National Economic and Social Forum and the National Agreements negotiated by the social partners provide for participation in developing the thinking that informs policy, in the negotiation of new policy commitments and in developing more effective approaches to policy implementation.

The engagement of the community and voluntary pillar as a social partner has allowed Traveller organisations access to these arenas. This access needs to be broadened to involve the participation of other minority ethnic organisations. This participation does produce outcomes; over the past decade the various arenas of social partnership have emerged as the key driving force for the institutional framework for equality that has been developed. This includes the new equality legislation, new equality institutions and a new focus on equality proofing. The most recent national agreement, the Programme for Prosperity and Fairness contains a range of important commitments in relation to racism, refugees and Travellers. The commitment by IBEC and ICTU in this agreement to preventing racism in the workplace is illustrative.

This commitment was further developed through a partnership involving the Equality Authority with IBEC, ICTU and the CIF. Anti-Racist Workplace Week was announced. A joint support pack was prepared identifying practical steps to ensure the workplace was anti-racist. During Anti-Racist Workplace Week, small scale initiatives were taken in enterprises across the country, and national and regional events were organised. This provided a valuable opportunity for the social partners to demonstrate a leadership in the fight against racism, and for a new consciousness to be developed at enterprise level of the need to take action on this issue.

Participation goes further than the arenas of social partnership. A social partnership ethos has gradually developed, whereby policy and provision are increasingly a product of consultation with, and participation by, relevant interests. This approach has increasingly involved black and minority ethnic people but needs further evolution and investment.

Mainstreaming and targeting
This notion of a social partnership ethos, an ethos that includes black and minority ethnic organisations, is central to another element of the necessary institutional framework to combat racism – mainstreaming. Mainstreaming is a term borrowed

from the European Union, a term with many associated meanings – a scenario that is useful for consensus but one that does facilitate practical progress.

Mainstreaming is about placing equality considerations – anti-racist and intercultural considerations in this instance – at the heart of all decision making. This allows us to shape what we do, and how we approach what we do, in a manner that reflects intercultural and anti-racist objectives. Mainstreaming is about changing the way we do our business so that as a society all ethnic groups have a sense of belonging and ownership, and so that all cultures are accommodated and secure expression.

This understanding of mainstreaming involves four dimensions:

- clarity of objectives, with targets and timescales as appropriate, that address the situation of black and minority ethnic groups.
- a system of proofing decision making so that we can test out and address the impact of decisions on black and minority ethnic groups, and the contribution of decisions to objectives established.
- a means of securing the participation of black and minority ethnic groups in this proofing process.
- the collection of data adequate to assessing outcomes for black and minority ethnic people from mainstream policy and service provisions.

Clearly, this approach will involve a focus across the full spectrum of the equality agenda rather than being confined to black and minority ethnic groups. This makes its development even more challenging. An Equality-Working Group involving the social partners, the Equality Authority, state agencies and

Government Departments is being convened by the Department of Justice Equality and Law Reform to begin to meet this challenge. Models are to be developed in relation to planning at local authority level, and in education and training provision. This will hopefully realise the learning necessary for a wider application of this approach.

More significant developments are happening in relation to mainstreaming a focus on equality between women and men. This should also be a source of learning for the inclusion of black and minority ethnic groups. A European Union regulation requires gender mainstreaming within all measures funded under the Structural Funds. The Irish National Development Plan, currently being implemented, includes both structural funds and significant exchequer funding. Most measures in the Plan are required to make a contribution to gender equality and to be designed on foot of gender equality impact assessments. Clearly, this is a part of the institutional framework to combat racism that requires significant development before its contribution is made. Serious barriers remain, including:

• a lack of data on the situation, experience and baseline numbers of black and minority ethnic people. In this regard, the decision not to include an ethnic question in the next census is disappointing. However, the Programme for Prosperity and Fairness does include commitments that would enhance data collection around service provision.
• an absence of advocacy and support for equality proofing. Investment in independent organisations that would encourage and assist policy makers in pursuing this mainstreaming approach has yet to be made.
• the need to develop simple and practical models for equality proofing across a wide agenda including black and minority

ethnic groups, to build a capacity among decision makers to apply these models and to provide the necessary resources for their applications.

The Equality Authority has accorded a priority to assisting the development of this approach. It has sought to build a model that takes difference as its starting print, to develop a template to be applied in local authority planning and to develop profiles of the groups to be included which set out their difference in terms of identity, situation and experience.

The Strategic Management Initiative, which is being implemented to modernise the public sector, also holds potential to assist this mainstreaming approach. Human resources, quality customer service and performance management themes within the Strategic Management Initiative have the potential to place anti-racist and intercultural objectives at the heart of public sector management. Already, work in the area of human resources has begun to focus on an equal opportunities policy that will assist greater diversity among civil servants. Equality and diversity have been defined as an underpinning principle for quality customer service, and the Equality Authority has assisted in preparing a pack to support the practical expression of this principle in public sector service provision. Further work is required in the area of performance management.

Targeting is more developed as an approach to anti-racism than mainstreaming. It is important to acknowledge that mainstreaming does not preclude targeting resources into black and minority ethnic communities and into activities to combat racism. Examples of current resourcing includes the creation of the National Consultative Committee on Racism and Interculturalism, the investment of resources into a new campaign to raise awareness of racism and anti-racism, and the development of an infrastructure to support the integration of refugees.

Targeting resources on Black and minority ethnic people has an important contribution to make. It is necessary to address the impact of past and current discrimination. It is required to meet culturally specific needs and aspirations. It also has a contribution to make to effective mainstreaming. Targeted measures provide learning that should inform and shape mainstream policy and provision. Equally these measures can create the conditions for effective participation by black and minority ethnic people in mainstream provision.

Rights and institutions

Mainstreaming and targeting are not currently underpinned by any legislative obligation. In Northern Ireland, however, the Northern Ireland Act places a statutory duty on public sector bodies to promote equality. The Equality Commission for Northern Ireland plays a significant role in supporting this duty. Public sector bodies are required to produce equality schemes for approval by the Commission. Key policy measures are subject to an equality impact assessment. These schemes and assessment cover a range of grounds including black and minority ethnic communities. This important development could usefully be deployed north and south. This is possible, given its origins in the Belfast Agreement, which also commits to an equivalence of rights north and south.

Legislated rights are an important element of the institutional framework required to combat racism. Rights covering black and minority ethnic groups, including a specific focus on Travellers, have evolved significantly in recent times in the south. An Employment Equality Act was passed in 1998 and an Equal Status Act in 2000. Both Acts prohibit discrimination across the nine grounds of gender, marital status, family status,

188 RESPONDING TO RACISM IN IRELAND

age, sexual orientation, disability, religion, race and membership of the Traveller community.

Direct and indirect discrimination are prohibited. Direct discrimination is defined in terms of less favourable treatment. Indirect discrimination is defined in terms of less favourable impact due to terms or conditions set that significantly disadvantage a particular group and that are not necessary.

Sexual harassment and harassment are also prohibited. Harassment is conduct based on one of the grounds that is unwelcome and that could be seen to be offensive, intimidating or humiliating.

The Employment Equality Act covers the workplace including recruitment, promotion, working conditions, equal pay, job advertisements, dismissal and access to vocational training. The Equal Status Act covers the provisions of goods, services and facilities, accommodation, education and the operation of registered clubs. The legislation is complex and contains a range of exemptions. However, it reflects a significant, coherent and holistic body of rights that are at the core of building an anti-racist and intercultural society. It is also a body of rights that will be further evolved once the new European Union 'Race Directive' is transposed into Irish Law.

The legislation creates two new bodies. The Office of the Director of Equality Investigations is established as the court where most cases under the Legislation are heard. The Equality Authority is established with the broad mandate to combat discrimination and to promote equality in the areas covered by the legislation. It has key responsibility for ensuring rights established are implemented.

The Equality Authority has sought to combine developmental and enforcement approaches in its work. In this way it is hoped to assist in realising not just the obligations set out in the legislation but the very ambitions that inspired the legislation.

The work of the Equality Authority is organised around three objectives:

1 To promote and defend the rights established: This involves providing information and advice on the legislation and legal support for cases of strategic importance. It also involves a communication strategy designed to build a consciousness of rights and obligations under the legislation, and a confidence in exercising those rights.

2 To support the development of a capacity to realise equality outcomes: This involves preparing codes of practice, conducting research, and developing practical equality initiatives. Much of this work is based on partnership with the relevant interests.

3 To contribute to a mainstreaming of equality: This involves a programme of equality reviews and action plans. These examine the equality situation in an organisation covering policy, perceptions, practices and procedures. Once examined, new goals are set and actions defined to meet these goals. It also involves work with the media, with the education system and a contribution to policy formulation.

A significant challenge facing the Equality Authority is how to advance the nine different grounds of the equality agenda in a manner that:

- ensures visibility across all grounds.
- reflects the salience of the gender ground.
- acknowledges the diversity between and within grounds.

Meeting this challenge effectively is vital to the effectiveness of the anti-racist work of the Equality Authority.

The Equality Authority has pursued an integrated approach involving three levels. One level involves a focus on individual grounds, such as the work done on organising the anti-racist workplace week. Another level involves initiatives that bring forward all nine grounds simultaneously. One example is the work described earlier in developing a pack to support an equality/diversity principle within quality customer service under the Strategic Management Initiative. At this level, anti-racism and interculturalism must be a feature of all Equality Authority initiatives. A third level involves an acknowledgement of the multiple identities held by most people, and developing initiatives off the situation of people holding multiple identities. At this level the focus could include the situation of minority ethnic women, black gay people or Travellers with a disability, among others.

Conclusion

The institutional framework detailed is that which is evolving at a national level. However, the elements of agenda and participation, mainstreaming and targeting, rights and institutions can, and need to, be replicated at local level and within individual organisations.

By way of conclusion, it is useful to set our what these elements might involve within an organisation. The elements could cover the whole equality agenda, but for current purposes they are detailed from an anti-racist perspective. As such an organisation wishing to be anti-racist and intercultural might be expected to have:

- an equality policy that incorporates an anti-racist position in relation to employment and operation strategies.
- a named person with responsibility for ensuring implementation of the policy.
- data collection and analysis to assess and monitor the outcomes of the equality policy.

- anti-racism training provided to all staff with particular attention to those responsible for policy making and for recruitment.
- positive action initiatives to outreach to black and minority ethnic communities, to address needs specific to these communities and to address any particular disadvantage that serves as a barrier to their participation.
- activities and approaches that build an organisational culture that openly values and accommodates cultural diversity and that communicates this outside the organisation.
- initiatives that create links with black and minority ethnic groups that ensure good communication and assist in a clarity about their situation and aspirations.

This institutional framework is only slowly emerging at the different levels. The foundations are in place. The commitment and participation of all sectors in society is now required to build on these foundations, so that an intercultural society gains greater definition, and becomes a reality.